CRITICAL PERSPECTIVES ON
HEALTH CARE

ANALYZING THE ISSUES

CRITICAL PERSPECTIVES ON
HEALTH CARE

Edited by Bridey Heing

Enslow Publishing

101 W. 23rd Street
Suite 240
New York, NY 10011
USA

enslow.com

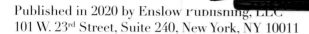

Published in 2020 by Enslow Publishing, LLC
101 W. 23rd Street, Suite 240, New York, NY 10011

Library of Congress Cataloging-in-Publication Data

Names: Heing, Bridey, editor.
Title: Critical perspectives on health care / edited by Bridey Heing.
Description: New York : Enslow Publishing, 2020. | Series: Analyzing the
issues | Audience: Grade 7-12. | Includes bibliographical references and
index.
Identifiers: LCCN 2018024472| ISBN 9781978503298 (library bound) | ISBN
9781978505001 (pbk.)
Subjects: LCSH: Medical policy—United States—Juvenile literature. |
Medical care—United States—Juvenile literature. | Health care reform—
United States.
Classification: LCC RA395.A3 C855 2019 | DDC 362.10973—dc23
LC record available at https://lccn.loc.gov/2018024472

Printed in the United States of America

To Our Readers: We have done our best to make sure all website addresses
in this book were active and appropriate when we went to press. However,
the author and the publisher have no control over and assume no
liability for the material available on those websites or on any websites
they may link to. Any comments or suggestions can be sent by email to
customerservice@enslow.com.

Excerpts and articles have been reproduced with the permission of the
copyright holders.

Photo Credits: Cover Monkey Business Images/Shutterstock.com; cover
and interior pages graphics Thaiview/Shutterstock.com (cover top,
pp. 3, 6–7), gbreezy/Shutterstock.com (magnifying glass), Ghornstern/
Shutterstock.com (chapter openers).

CONTENTS

INTRODUCTION

Few policy issues have inspired the kinds of debate and passion that health care has in the past decade. Defined by strong partisan lines and high-powered advocacy groups, the way we provide health care to American citizens inspires difficult conversations and often times even more difficult policy choices. In recent years it has also been difficult to separate fact from hyperbole, and the debate has become harder and harder to understand in its entirety.

The health care debate is not new. Since the mid-twentieth century, leaders and advocates have fought for greater access to medical care. The cost of health care has ballooned in the past few decades, due in part to costs imposed by insurance companies and by the way billing is administered by hospitals. But millions are unable to afford out-of-pocket costs, either for insurance coverage or to self-insure. For those who find themselves in need of care with inadequate coverage, bankruptcy is a very real threat, while others have foregone necessary and life saving care as a result of the associated costs.

These issues have led to legislation. In 1965, Medicaid and Medicare were passed by Congress, offering support for the elderly and low-income families who struggled to pay for medical expenses.

In 1997, the Children's Health Insurance Program (CHIP) was introduced to offer further assistance to minors based on state-set guidelines. In 2010, the Affordable Care Act (ACA) was signed into law, becoming one of the most sweeping pieces of legislation ever passed in regard to health care. In addition to creating health market exchanges and putting restrictions on insurance companies in relation to issues like pre-existing conditions, it imposed an individual mandate that requires all citizens to have insurance through a company or through a federal program.

At its heart, this is a debate about ensuring people have the care they need to stay safe and healthy. That's why it inspires such heated debate — everyone, at some point, needs to have access to effective and affordable medical help. This collection seeks to explore all angles of this debate, so that readers can have a foundation to understand the way our understanding of health care has evolved over time and will continue to change moving forward.

CHAPTER 1

WHAT THE EXPERTS SAY

Health care is a complicated subject, with many factors that play a role in access and quality of care. This makes research all the more important; experts and scholars can help us understand how gender, race, location, and income influences the way we find, use, and engage with medical services. Experts can also give us a sense of how other models, such as those in other countries, might apply to the US health care system and help find innovative and reasonable solutions to issues facing our health care system. But health care is also a highly controversial topic, with many ideas about the best ways to ensure we all have access to the care we need. That means that we must be aware of the sources of research we look to for fair and balanced information.

"EXPLAINER: WHY CAN'T ANYONE TELL ME HOW MUCH THIS SURGERY WILL COST?," BY BETSY Q. CLIFF, FROM *THE CONVERSATION*, JANUARY 12, 2016

Thanks to rising annual deductibles and a push toward consumer-driven health care, people are increasingly encouraged to shop around for medical care. Many states or state hospital associations have price transparency initiatives, and there are a number of private companies that also purport to help consumers find value for their health care dollar.

But the search for the best price is often stymied, not necessarily by a lack of information, but by a lack of *relevant* information.

Price in health care is a squishy concept. Different words relating to cost – charge, price and out-of-pocket cost – all have different meanings and there is no standard among consumer transparency websites about which of these prices to report. So, while the price variation between hospitals is well-recognized, less often discussed is that when consumers search for price, the variation in information reported means they may see wide variation within the same hospital for the same procedure. The lack of standards in this respect can leave consumers confused and means some price transparency efforts may be doing more harm than good.

SEARCHING FOR A PRICE

As an example of how confusing things can get, in mid-December 2015 I searched for the price of spinal fusion surgery, a common procedure, at a hospital near my Michigan home, the Henry Ford Health System.

My first stop was the website run by the Michigan Health & Hospital Association, the trade association representing hospitals in the state. There, I found out that the average charge at Henry Ford was about US$71,000. Then I looked for other sources of price information for consumers. The first result that came up in a Google search for "compare hospital prices" was a site called OpsCost. That site showed me a billed price of about $67,000 at Henry Ford and also told me Medicare reimbursed about $33,000 for the procedure. I looked for something on the site that would explain why there was a difference between these numbers, and how they relate to other insurers, but couldn't find it.

Then, I tried Healthcare Bluebook, which allowed me to narrow into a zip code but not a specific hospital. That website said that the "fair price" for my spinal fusion procedure in the zip code where Henry Ford is located would be about $39,000. I tried another, Fair Health, which also let me search just by zip code. That website said my procedure cost $9,350.

It's easy to see how a well-intentioned consumer would get frustrated.

WHY IS THERE SO MUCH VARIATION?

None of the prices in the above examples are wrong, per se. They just give the cost of different things. And, most importantly, none of them likely reflect the cost that someone with insurance would pay for the procedure.

The first two examples, from the hospital association and OpsCost, show the billed, or chargemaster, amounts at Henry Ford. That is akin to a "sticker price" for the service. It is rare that anyone with health insurance would pay an amount that high if the hospital is included in their insurer's network. Just as a car buyer might haggle down from the sticker price of a vehicle, an insurance company negotiates a lower price for its members.

People with insurance pay less than the charge-master amount, but it's hard to tell just how much less. This is known as the negotiated price, or sometimes the actual paid amount. In some instances, the insurer pays very close to the chargemaster price, while in others they pay much less. That can vary based on the insurer or by the hospital, making the chargemaster price virtually meaningless for comparing hospital prices for those with commercial insurance.

The prices quoted by Healthcare Bluebook and Fair Health are both meant to estimate actual amounts paid by insurers to hospitals. These prices are disclosed in an explanation of benefits statement (it's the amount after the insurance discount is removed), but you usually don't see that until after the procedure is done and you get the statement.

The negotiated price is usually a closely guarded secret. Because of this fact, the websites do not have or do not reveal Henry Ford's or any other hospitals' actual negotiated prices. So unless you know someone with the same insurance who just had done the same procedure at the same hospital, you'd have a hard time finding that number. In addition, neither website asked about the generosity of my insurance benefit, which determines my out-of-pocket cost, the actual amount I would owe.

Then, there's the issue of what is encompassed in the quoted price, which is likely the source of the large discrepancy between what Fair Health reported as a fair cost ($9,350) and what Healthcare Bluebook reported ($39,000). Healthcare Bluebook estimated the hospital's facility fee, physician fee and anesthesia fee based on typical recovery time and prices. The Fair Health price is a bit unclear, but it seems to include only the price of the actual surgery, not taking anesthesia or the cost of the hospital stay into account.

What if you don't have insurance? In some cases, patients are billed chargemaster prices. However, many hospitals will work with these people to lower large bills. Additionally, thanks to the Affordable Care Act, anyone without insurance who is eligible for financial assistance must be billed a lower amount, usually based on average insurer payments. Uninsured people with higher incomes may still pay chargemaster prices within the law.

The best thing you can do if you know you have a major medical expense coming up is call your insurer. Most large insurers now have tools that help consumers shop around for health care providers, and they can often give you an idea of the variation in costs you would face at different providers in your network and specific to your plan.

Next, as a policy recommendation, we need to be careful about releasing information on billed charges under the guise of price transparency, and particularly about calling these numbers prices. They bear little relevance to what the vast majority of consumers will pay and simply distract from finding relevant information on actual prices facing patients.

Price transparency is undoubtedly hard to implement. But it doesn't have to be as hard as we are making it.

1. How does variable pricing impact health care in the United States?

2. Would not knowing pricing make people more or less likely to seek care? Why or why not?

EXCERPT FROM "SURVEY DISSECTS U.S. HEALTHCARE SPENDING OVER THE DECADES," BY DAVID TRILLING, FROM *JOURNALIST'S RESOURCE*, JANUARY 12, 2017

Diabetes, heart disease and back pain are the priciest ailments in the United States, a new survey has found. And the cost of healthcare is rising faster than inflation.

The issue: Americans spend more on healthcare per capita than any other nation — roughly 10 times the global average, says the World Health Organization. The amount is growing. According to U.S. government figures, healthcare spending leapt 5.8 percent in 2015 – as the Affordable Care Act expanded coverage – to reach $3.2 trillion or an average of $9,990 per person. All told, healthcare accounts for 17.8 percent of the economy.

But little is known about exactly how the money is spent. A new survey seeks to shed light on the outlays, to determine how spending is changing over time, and to identify the most expensive ailments. Such information could help drive investments in new cures and help policymakers understand where to focus attention.

An academic study worth reading: "U.S. Spending on Personal Health Care and Public Health, 1996-2013," in *JAMA*, December 2016.

Study summary: A team led by Joseph Dieleman of the University of Washington looked at 183 sources of nationally representative data (including government budgets, insurance claims, a variety of national surveys and the government's National Health Expenditure Data) to examine spending on 155 conditions, including 29 types of cancer, from 1996 to 2013. They sought to comprehensively estimate personal and public healthcare spending by condition, age and gender, and type of care.

Dieleman and colleagues grouped spending into six categories: inpatient care, ambulatory care (visits to a doctor's office and outpatient treatment at hospitals), emergency care, nursing facilities, dentistry and prescriptions. Other spending included over-the-counter medicines, medical devices and house calls.

For public health spending by the government, the researchers examined audited appropriations for the "four primary federal agencies providing public health funding: the Health Resources and Services Administration, the Centers for Disease Control and Prevention [CDC], the Substance Abuse and Mental Health Services Administration, and the U.S. Food and Drug Administration [FDA]."

FINDINGS:

- The costliest illness in 2013 was diabetes. Spending on diabetes totaled an estimated $101.4 billion. Roughly 57.6 percent of this figure was spent on prescription pharmaceuticals. Between 1996 and 2013, spending on diabetes increased by 6.1 percent per year.

- The second-costliest condition was heart disease, at $88.1 billion. About 56.5 percent of this spending was on inpatient care; 61.2 percent was spent on adults aged 65 years or older. Between 1996 and 2013, spending on heart disease increased an average of 0.2 percent annually.
- Low back and neck pain was the third-highest category, at an estimated $87.6 billion – largely on ambulatory (outpatient/walk-in) care.
- Of all conditions, those with the fastest increase in spending were autistic spectrum disorders (17.6 percent), Vitamin A deficiency (14.7 percent), high cholesterol (10.3 percent) and obesity (9.9 percent).
- Personal health spending (money spent on individual care) in 2013 totaled $2.1 trillion.
- The costliest cancers were colon and rectum cancers, at $18.5 billion. The cost increased by 2 percent per year between 1996 and 2013.
- Females spent 24.6 percent more than males overall in 2013. Spending on females was greater than males for ages 15 to 64 and above age 74.
- Excluding infants, spending per person generally increases with age.
- Between 1996 and 2013 healthcare spending increased between 3 percent and 4 percent per year; spending on pharmaceuticals increased, on average, by 5.6 percent annually. (By comparison, average inflation during that period was 4 percent, according to the Federal Reserve Bank of Minneapolis.)
- Personal health spending increased for 143 of 155 conditions between 1996 and 2013.
- Personal health spending comprised 89.5 percent of total health spending in 2013. Other spending was largely federal support for organizations like the CDC and the FDA.

- The three conditions that received the most federal health spending were HIV/AIDS ($3.5 billion), lower respiratory tract infections ($1.8 billion), and diarrheal diseases ($0.9 billion). [...]

HELPFUL RESOURCES:

A number of government and multilateral organizations publish data on health spending in the U.S., including the World Health Organization, the federal Centers for Medicare and Medicaid Services, the National Institutes of Health, the CDC's National Center for Health Statistics, and the Department of Health and Human Services, which operates the Agency for Healthcare Research and Quality.

1. Based on these findings, how would you characterize personal health care costs?

"REIMAGINING THE FUTURE OF AMERICA'S HEALTH CARE SYSTEM," BY ADRIENNE DAWSON, FROM TEXAS ENTERPRISE AT THE UNIVERSITY OF TEXAS, MAY 3, 2017

Dr. Mark McClellan agrees that iPads, air travel, and endless cable channels are great, but what people really value, he says, are longer and better lives. We want "the time to enjoy all of those things."

The health care industry is responding. Worldwide increases in productivity in the health care system exceed the value of productivity increases of every other sector of the economy combined. But McClellan, senior policy advisor for Dell Medical School, points out that as productivity increases, so must the amount of money budgeted to pay for medical services, treatments, and therapies. Case in point, the U.S. government spends money on three main budget categories: social security, health care — and last, says, McClellan, "everything else."

McClellan, MD, Ph.D., also serves as the director of the Margolis Center for Health Policy at Duke University and is the former head of the FDA and Centers for Medicare and Medicaid Services.

"Health care spending was 1 percent of GDP in the '70s, it's 5 percent of GDP today, and it's on track according to the Congressional Budget Office to be 8 to 9 percent of GDP over the next 20 years," he says. "Just for perspective, the $600 billion we'll spend on defense and homeland security is about a third less than is budgeted this year for my former agency, the CMS [Centers for Medicare and Medicaid]."

DIVERGENCE IN POPULATION OUTCOMES

When it comes to health care in the U.S., McClellan emphasizes that the problem isn't the amount spent. "The one constant in U.S. macroeconomic policy over the last 40-plus years is that when there's been a choice between spending more on health care and spending more on just about any other programs, health care wins."

The problem, he says, is in the distribution of funds.

Compared to 34 other nations in the Organisation for Economic Cooperation and Development (OECD), the United States' health care spending is on par with its peers. Where things diverge is how those funds are allocated. "In the OECD, for every dollar spent on health care, about two dollars are spent on social services," McClellan explains.

Conversely, the U.S. spends about half as much on social services as it does for traditional health care programs.

As a result, we're witnessing a divergence in population health outcomes. That means that even though people value longer and better lives, there's an increase in mortality rates related to substance abuse, violence, suicide, cardiovascular disease, diabetes, and cancer. These things had been trending downward for the last century in developed nations, he says, but are now on the rise among certain U.S. demographic subsections, particularly white, middle-aged, low-to-middle-income Americans.

"The big story with premature death," McClellan stresses, "are behavioral issues and social and environmental factors, the things that are more likely to be addressed by those other types of programs that have consistently been squeezed down in federal and state spending over the last 30 or 40 years."

FEE-FOR-VALUE, NOT FEE-FOR-SERVICE

But along with the unceasing and often contentious debates — and stalemate — surrounding the Affordable Care Act is how to keep moving forward to address these very coverage issues given increasing health care costs. McClellan says that's why more interest needs to be taken in addressing the value of care.

McClellan and National Academy of Medicine President Victor Dzau recently released a study that looks beyond policy debates to improve the nation's health care system. A key element, he says, is moving from a fee-for-service model to a fee-for-value approach.

But as new biomedical advancements become available to treat diseases from HIV and hepatitis to cancer, the costs for those treatments rise. They're more valuable — they lead to longer and better lives — but they're also more expensive. The opportunity, he says, is for improving how those treatments are delivered. For many patients, using home health services, telemedicine, and more social service support would not only be more effective, it would also be cheaper.

"For those with more limited means or complex conditions, it isn't so much the health care access that's the root cause of the health problem, it's things like access to housing or access to support services for behavioral health or substance abuse problems or other things that typically occur outside of the traditional health care setting," he adds.

The challenge is that in our traditional health care system, those forms of care aren't reimbursed. McClellan advocates moving to a fee structure that pays health practitioners for achieving the desired health outcome, not simply for ordering a test or scan. That gives clinicians the freedom to make decisions that are in the best interest of the patient. They're able to make treatment options available that are often less expensive and more effective, all while being compensated for achieving the ultimate goal: Giving people longer and better lives.

1. How does US health care spending compare to other developed countries?

2. What is the difference between fee-for-value and fee-for-service models of health care?

EXCERPT FROM "THE IMPACT OF PRIMARY CARE: A FOCUSED REVIEW," BY LEIYU SHI, FROM *SCIENTIFICA*, NOVEMBER 8, 2012

ABSTRACT

Primary care serves as the cornerstone in a strong healthcare system. However, it has long been overlooked in the United States (USA), and an imbalance between specialty and primary care exists. The objective of this focused review paper is to identify research evidence on the value of primary care both in the USA and internationally, focusing on the importance of effective primary care services in delivering quality healthcare, improving health outcomes, and reducing disparities. Literature searches were performed in PubMed as well as "snowballing" based on the bibliographies of the retrieved articles. The areas reviewed included primary care definitions, primary care measurement, primary care practice, primary care and health, primary care and quality, primary care and cost, primary care and equity, primary care and health centers, and primary care and healthcare reform. In both developed and developing countries, primary care has been demonstrated to be associated with enhanced access to healthcare services, better health outcomes, and a decrease in hospitalization and use of emergency department visits. Primary care can also help counteract the negative impact of poor economic conditions on health.

1. INTRODUCTION

Primary care serves as the cornerstone for building a strong healthcare system that ensures positive health outcomes and health equity [1, 2]. In the past century, there has been a transition in healthcare from focusing on disease-oriented etiologies to examining the interacting influences of factors rooted in culture, race/ethnicity, policy, and environment. Such a transition called for person/family-focused and community-oriented primary care services to be provided in a continuous and coordinated manner in order to meet the health needs of the population. In 2001, the World Health Organization (WHO) proposed a global goal of achieving universal primary care in the six domains established by the 1978 Alma-Ata Declaration: first contact, longitudinality, comprehensiveness, coordination, person or family-centeredness, and community orientation. These six attributes, agreed upon internationally, have proved effective in identifying breadth of primary care services and monitoring primary care quality [3, 6].

However, despite near consensus around the world that primary care is a critical component of any healthcare system, there is a considerable imbalance between primary and specialty care in the United States (USA) and many other parts of the world. For example, in the USA, in 2008, among 954,224 total doctors of medicine, 784,199 were actively practicing and 305,264 were practicing in primary care specialties (32% of the total and 39% of actively practicing physicians) [7]. The proportion of specialists was over 60% of all patient care physicians.

The major driving force behind the increasing number of medical specialists is the development of medical technology. The rapid advances in medical technology continuously expanded the diagnostic and therapeutic options at the disposal of physician specialists.

The majority of patients, significantly freed from financial constraints thanks to third-party insurance payment, have turned to physicians who can provide them with the most up-to-date, sophisticated treatment. Hence, the rapid advance of medical technology contributes to the demand for specialty services and provides an impetus for further specialty development.

In addition, significantly higher insurance reimbursement for specialists relative to primary care physicians also contributes to the current imbalance. Under the resource-based relative value scale (RBRVS), implemented for US Medicare physician payment, primary care physicians continue to receive lower payments than specialists for comparable work because physician payments are based on historically determined, estimated practice costs as well as total work effort [8, 9]. Moreover, many insurance companies will pay for hospital-based complex diagnostic and invasive procedures using high technology, but not for routine preventive visits and consultations. Such practices not only encourage medical students' career choices in subspecialties and practicing physicians' provision of intensive specialty services, but also discourage the provision of important primary care services and deter patients from early care-seeking behavior.

Specialist physicians enjoy other benefits as well. Not only do specialists earn significantly higher incomes than primary care physicians, but also they are more likely to have predictable work hours and enjoy higher prestige both among their colleagues and from the public at large [10, 11]. Problems typically cited in recruiting primary care physicians include longer working hours during the day as well as on call, less financial reward for service, and less access to the highly technological approaches to diagnosis which is an important part of the medical center approach to patient care [12]. Among factors affecting medical students' career choice, society's perception of value, intellectual challenge, and lifestyle factors (e.g., hours worked) were ranked as very important along with financial reward [13–15]. The medical education environment, organized according to specialties and controlled largely by those who have achieved their leadership positions by demonstrating their ability in narrow scientific or clinical areas, emphasizes technology intensive procedures, and tertiary care settings also deter the choice by students of primary care specialties [16, 17].

Perhaps the most important reason for this imbalance is the lack of appreciation for the true value of primary care. Relative to disease-specific research, primary care-oriented studies have been relatively few. Their dissemination and recognition within the medical field are also problematic. Policymakers and the general public also have little knowledge of the efficacy of primary care, its impact on individual and population health, and its role in today's healthcare delivery. These realities have led to superfluous political commitments and the disengagement of related sectors [18, 19]. A WHO 2000 report announced that primary care has failed to serve as the foundation of care for all people [2].

The objective of this focused review paper is to present the research findings regarding the efficacy of primary care so that the value of primary care can be better appreciated. Specifically, it will demonstrate the importance of effective primary care services in delivering quality healthcare, improving health outcomes, and reducing disparities. [...]

2.1. PRIMARY CARE DEFINITIONS

The terms "primary care" and "primary healthcare" describe two different concepts. The former, primary care, refers to family medicine services typically provided by physicians to individual patients and is person-oriented, longitudinal care. Primary healthcare, in contrast, is a broader concept intended to describe both individual-level care and population-focused activities that incorporate public health elements. In addition, primary healthcare may include broader societal policies such as universal access to healthcare, an emphasis on health equity, and collaboration within and beyond the medical sector [20].

Primary care plays a central role in a healthcare delivery system. Other essential levels of care include secondary and tertiary care, which encompass different roles within the health spectrum. Compared to primary care, secondary and tertiary care services are more complex and specialized, and the types of care are further distinguished according to duration, frequency, and level of intensity. Secondary care is usually short-term, involving sporadic consultation from a specialist to provide expert opinion and/or surgical or other advanced interventions that primary care physicians (PCPs) are not equipped to perform. Secondary care thus includes hospitalization, routine surgery, specialty consultation, and rehabilitation. Tertiary care is the most complex level of care, needed for conditions that are relatively uncommon. Typically, tertiary care is institution-based, highly specialized, and technology-driven. Much of tertiary care is rendered in large teaching hospitals, especially university-affiliated teaching hospitals. Examples include trauma care, burn treatment, neonatal intensive care, tissue transplants, and open heart surgery. In some instances, tertiary treatment may be extended, and the tertiary care physician may assume long-term responsibility for the bulk of the patient's care. It has been estimated that 75% to 85% of people in a general population require only primary care services in a given year; 10% to 12% require referrals to short-term secondary care services; 5% to 10% use tertiary care specialists [21].

Since its introduction in 1961, the term primary care has been defined in various ways, often using one or more of the following categories of classification [4, 22–24]. These categories include the following.

(i) The care provided by certain clinicians, the Clinton administration's Health Security Act, for example, specified primary care as family medicine, general internal medicine, general pediatrics, and obstetrics and gynecology. Some experts and groups have also included nurse practitioners and physician assistants.

(ii) A set of activities whose functions act as the boundaries of primary care—such as curing or alleviating common illnesses and disabilities.

(iii) A level of care or setting—an entry point to a system that also includes secondary care (by community hospitals) and tertiary care (by medical centers and teaching hospitals).

(iv) A set of attributes, as in the 1978 IOM definition—care that is accessible, comprehensive, coordinated, continuous, and accountable—or as defined by Starfield—care that is characterized by first contact, accessibility, longitudinality, and comprehensiveness.

(v) A strategy for organizing the healthcare system as a whole—such as community-oriented primary care, which gives priority and resources to community-based healthcare while placing less emphasis on hospital-based, technology-intensive, and acute-care medicine.

Definitions of primary care often focus on the type or level of services, such as prevention, diagnostic and therapeutic services, health education and counseling, and minor surgery. Although primary care specifically emphasizes these services, many specialists also provide the same spectrum of services. For example, the practice of most ophthalmologists has a large element of prevention, as well as diagnosis, treatment, followup, and minor surgery. Similarly, most cardiologists are engaged in health education and counseling. Hence, according to some experts, primary care should be more appropriately viewed as an approach to providing healthcare, rather than as a set of specific services [21].

The World Health Organization (WHO) describes primary care as essential healthcare based on practical, scientifically sound, and socially acceptable methods and technology made universally accessible to individuals and families in the community by means acceptable to them and at a cost that the community and the country can afford to maintain at every stage of their development in a spirit of self-reliance and self-determination. It forms an integral part of both the country's health system (of which it is the central function) and a main focus of the overall social and economic development of the community. It is the first level of contact for individuals, the family, and the community with the national health system, bringing healthcare as close as possible to where people live and work, and constitutes the first element of a continuing healthcare process [25].

Others define primary care as the health services rendered by providers acting as the principal point of consultation for patients within a healthcare system [26, 27]. This provider could be a primary care physician, such as a general practitioner or family physician, or (depending on the locality, health system organization, and the patient's discretion) a pharmacist, a physician assistant, a nurse practitioner, a nurse (as is common in the United Kingdom), a clinical officer (such as in parts of Africa), or an Ayurvedic or other traditional medicine professionals (such as in parts of Asia). Depending on the nature of the health condition, patients may then be referred for secondary or tertiary care.

Perhaps the most comprehensive definition of primary care was given by Starfield in her landmark book *Primary care: balancing health needs, services and technology* [4]; Starfield defined primary care as the provision of integrated, accessible healthcare services by clinicians who are accountable for addressing a large majority of personal healthcare needs, developing a sustained partnership with patients, and practicing in the context of family and community. She summarized the following characteristics of primary care (pp. 19–34).

(i) Integrated care is intended to encompass the provision of comprehensive, coordinated, and continuous services that provide a seamless process of care. Integration combines information about events occurring in disparate settings and levels of care as well as over time, preferably throughout the life span.

(ii) Comprehensive care addresses any health problem at any given stage of a patient's life cycle.

(iii) Coordinated care ensures the provision of a combination of health services and information to meet a patient's needs. It also refers to the connection between, or the rational ordering of, those services, including the resources of the community.

(iv) Continuous care is a characteristic that refers to care over time by a single individual or team of healthcare professionals ("clinician continuity") as well as to effective and timely maintenance and communication of health information (events, risks, advice, and patient preferences) ("record continuity").

(v) Accessible care refers to the ease with which a patient can initiate an interaction for any health problem with a clinician (e.g., by phone or at a treatment location) and includes efforts to eliminate barriers such as those posed by geography, administrative hurdles, financing, culture, and language.

(vi) Healthcare services refer to an array of services that are performed by healthcare professionals or under their direction, for the purpose of promoting, maintaining, or restoring health. The term refers to all settings of care (such as hospitals, nursing homes, physicians' offices, intermediate care facilities, schools, and homes).

(vii) A clinician is an individual who uses a recognized scientific knowledge base and has the authority to direct the delivery of personal health services to patients.

(viii) Accountability is applied to primary care clinicians and the systems in which they operate. These clinicians and systems are responsible to their patients and communities for addressing a large majority of personal health needs through a sustained partnership with a patient in the context of a family and community and for (1) quality of care, (2) patient satisfaction, (3) efficient use of resources, and (4) ethical behavior.

(ix) A majority of personal healthcare needs refer to the essential characteristic of primary care clinicians: that they receive all problems that patients bring—unrestricted by problem or organ system—and have the appropriate training to manage a large majority of those problems, involving other practitioners for further evaluation or treatment when appropriate. Personal healthcare needs include physical, mental, emotional, and social concerns that involve the functioning of an individual.

(x) Sustained partnership refers to the relationship established between the patient and clinician with the mutual expectation of continuation over time. It is predicated on the development of mutual trust, respect, and responsibility.

(xi) A patient is an individual who interacts with a clinician either because of real or perceived illness or for health promotion and disease prevention.

(xii) Context of family and community refers to an understanding of the patient's living conditions, family dynamics, and cultural background. Community refers to the population served, whether they are patients or not. It can refer to a geopolitical boundary (a city, county, or state), members of a health plan, or neighbors who share values, experiences, language, religion, culture, or ethnic heritage.

2.2. PRIMARY CARE MEASUREMENT

Measurement enables assessment of the performance of a healthcare delivery system and individual providers. Additionally, measurement facilitates efforts to improve accountability, quality, appropriate use of resources, and patient outcomes and to lower the risk of adverse events [28]. Measurement is also increasingly tied to healthcare financing through pay-for-performance programs. As the USA attempts to emphasize primary care functions through aspects of the Patient Protection and Affordable Care Act [29], measurement of primary care will take on even greater importance. Shi notes that assessments of the quality of primary care patients receive should consider the four dimensions of primary care: the first contact experience, longitudinality, coordination, and comprehensiveness [30].

Researchers can use various types of indicators depending on the goal of measurement [28]. Indicators can provide some sense of the structure, process, or outcome of care, can be used to measure activity, performance, and quality, and can help determine whether the care is being provided according to guidelines specified by an expert body or consensus [28].

The Primary Care Assessment Tool (PCAT) is a collection of questionnaires, developed by Johns Hopkins Primary Care Policy Center under the leadership of the late Dr. Barbara Starfield, that assess whether a healthcare provider or system is achieving the four core functions of primary care (first contact, longitudinality, comprehensiveness, and coordination) and three supplementary aspects of primary care (family centeredness, community orientation, and cultural competence). The first PCAT-adult questionnaire was developed and validated in the USA [31, 32] but its validity and reliability have been demonstrated in other countries, such as in Brazil [33] and Spain [34]. Several forms of the PCAT exist, varying in length and target population. For example, while the Primary Care Assessment Tool-Adult Edition's (PCAT-AE) original form includes 74 items assessing adult patient experiences with primary care [31, 32] a short 10-item version, the PCAT10-AE has also been used and integrated into a national population health survey [34]. A PCAT assessing the primary care experiences of children has been developed as well [33, 35]. In addition to these questionnaires targeting patients, versions of the PCAT have been developed that also survey providers and administrators of facilities, providing another perspective on the provision of primary care [36].

In addition to the PCAT collection of survey instruments, researchers have used other surveys to measure aspects of primary care provision from the patient and provider perspective in the USA and in international settings. These include the Health Tracking Physician Survey [37], the International Health Policy Survey [38], and the Ambulatory Care Experiences Survey [39]. Other studies have used claims data [40, 41] and medical record review [40, 42–44] to assess the quality, performance, and cost-effectiveness of primary care in various settings.

Medical experts have defined standards of practice for assessment of providers or facilities in terms of whether they are practicing according to recommended guidelines [38–44]. For example, a survey fielded in five countries determined that the USA performed well in delivering preventive care according to clinical guidelines [38], hypothesizing that this result might be due to third party insurers' increasing emphasis on quality measurement using tools such as the National Committee for Quality Assurance's (NCQA) Healthcare Effectiveness Data and Information Set (HEDIS). In addition to HEDIS, other indicators, such as the Diabetes Quality Improvement Project [40], have been developed to support measurement of the quality of care provided in a primary care setting for a particular condition. Many measures of performance and quality in the healthcare setting are disease-specific. Given primary care's emphasis on patient-centered and comprehensive care, these disease-specific measures may not be most useful for the primary care context. Other measurement efforts attempt to move beyond condition-specific indicators. Hospitalization for ambulatory care sensitive conditions (ACSC), defined as "diagnoses for which timely and effective outpatient care can help to reduce the risk of hospitalization" [45], has been proposed as a way to assess access to care and as an outcome measure of the effectiveness of prior primary care intervention [41]. However, research has shown that ACSC-related hospitalizations may occur too infrequently and be too difficult to link with previous receipt of primary care to serve as a viable outcome measure [41]. On the other hand, increased access to healthcare services is accomplished through expanded insurance coverage, thus also enabling greater financial access to hospital resources. Therefore, studies using preventable hospitalizations as outcome measures to examine the impacts of primary care access should consider how that improved access is being facilitated [46]. Another survey attempting to identify good indicators asked physicians about the types of patient outcomes that they value as good indicators of primary care providers' performance; respondents identified nineteen indicators related to patients' physical functioning, physical pain, physical symptoms besides pain, clinical indicators, emotional distress, health behaviors, and general quality of life.

Other literature examines the measurement of primary care with respect to unique populations, particular models of care, or atypical settings [39, 47, 48]. One challenge is measuring care provided to complex patients (patients with multiple chronic conditions), given that disease-specific measures are ill-suited for this population [48]. Therefore, indicators of the continuity and coordination aspects of primary care provision are particularly important for assessing the quality of care this complex population experiences [48]. Given the increasing emphasis on patient-centered medical homes (PCMH), measuring the impact of multidisciplinary teams (in contrast to individual providers) may better elucidate the patient experience of care in PCMH settings [39]. However, NCQA standards to assess medical homes may not be appropriate for all practice settings; for example, the military health system confronts different challenges when establishing medical homes related to deployment and the frequent movement of patients and providers. [47]

Finally, the facilitators and barriers to implementing quality measurement in primary care were systematically reviewed in a study on primary care in Canada. Content analysis of the 57 English-language articles published between 1996 and 2005 identified seven common categories of facilitators and barriers for implementing innovations, guidelines, and quality indicators. The authors found that successful implementation of quality measures can occur but that success depends on the interaction of multiple factors, including measurement characteristics, promotional messages, implementation strategies, resources, the intended adopters, and the intraorganizational and interorganizational contexts. Research has also found that the nature of the relationship between the patient and PCP impacts patients' perception of the quality of care they are receiving [50] and correlates positively with measures of primary care provider performance [51]. However, while the quality of care patients receive may be heavily impacted by the strength of connection patients feel with their providers, research has found that patients generally do not feel well connected to their PCPs [51].

In summary, primary care measurement includes tools that assess many aspects of care: the extent to which a primary care setting fulfills the major components of primary care; the performance of the provider or facility; the quality of care patients receive; how facets of care delivery, such as various models of care, team approaches, and different settings, impact care. Tools to collect data include primary data collection from surveys and secondary analysis using claims data and medical chart abstraction. Given the nature of primary care practice, indicators that are patient-centered rather than disease-specific are likely going to be increasingly important in enabling a more accurate assessment of the care patients receive.

2.3. PRIMARY CARE PRACTICE

Many countries place great emphasis on primary care and have developed strong primary care infrastructures [52–54]. Examples include Britain's National Health Service (NHS), which established Primary Care Trusts (PCT) that integrate primary and hospital-based care and comprise the bulk of the NHS budget [52, 55]. Canada has a more balanced primary care-specialist physician ratio than the USA with only 10% more specialists than primary care physicians, in contrast to over 50% more in the USA [56]. Developing countries, like Brazil and Thailand, have also implemented national-level strategies to increase access to primary care services [57, 58].

An increasingly popular model for orienting the healthcare system to primary care is the gatekeeper model, which requires patients to select a primary care physician (PCP) and then obtain referrals through that PCP to specialists [59]. However, gatekeeper models may meet resistance from medical professionals and consumers in some countries [60]. Therefore, efforts to promote gate keeping in a healthcare system should consider gradual, incentive-driven approaches [60].

In conjunction with acting, in some systems, as gatekeepers to more specialized services, PCPs also may serve as patients' point of first contact with the healthcare system. Many countries have expanded access to primary care by establishing call centers, flexible hours, and clinics. Spain, for example, has sought to make care accessible both in financial and geographic terms, by enacting universal insurance coverage and striving to make healthcare facilities available within fifteen minutes to every person in need [61].

Continuity of care is also promoted through structures such as medical homes or well-developed health information technology (health IT) systems. [59] In Spain, for example, nearly every resident has an identification card that enables providers to access their medical history and relevant information at an appointment or emergency [61]. These countries have also sought to raise the status of primary care by establishing the discipline as a specialty within medicine and instituting reforms to payment systems [59].

Team-based models of providing primary care and the connections of these models with quality are becoming increasingly important as insurers use pay-for-performance incentives in payment schemes [62]. In order to support high-functioning teams, the associations between team-level job satisfaction and performance should be explored, a relationship which may be affected by the status and support enjoyed by the PCPs in a setting [62]. Research also suggests that the functioning level of primary care teams may affect patient outcomes, with those patients cared for by high functioning primary care teams experiencing better health outcomes [63]. Team-based approaches to primary care may also facilitate integration of mental health and primary care. As an example, the USA-based Intermountain Healthcare's mental health integration system includes PCPs, psychiatrists, nurses, family members, and other parties to integrate mental health services into the usual practice of primary care [64].

Scope of practice, the extent of health insurance coverage in a region, ease of coordination with other sectors, and myriad other factors impact the way in which primary care is practiced in a country, region, or individual practice. Countries that have enacted reforms that build on their existing primary care infrastructures can serve as case studies for the USA, where the ongoing implementation of the Patient Protection and Affordable Care Act (ACA) seeks to enhance the role of primary care in the US healthcare system.

Currently, in contrast to some of its industrialized peers, the US healthcare system is much more heavily skewed toward specialty care [56, 58]. Although 51.3% of office visits were to primary care physicians in 2008, only about one-third of practicing physicians specialize in primary care [65]. A combination of primary care physicians, nurse practitioners (NPs), and physician assistants (PAs) comprise the estimated 400,000 primary care providers in the USA, with physicians contributing the largest portion (74%). Scopes of practice for NPs and PAs have broadened in many states in recent years, enabling these providers to take on more responsibilities in the provision of care. However, the distribution of primary care providers in the USA is uneven, with 5,902 communities designated as primary care health professional shortage areas [67].

Changes to the Medicare fee schedule (which had previously favored specialists in reimbursement rates) [68], support for Title VII health professions training programs [69, 70], and the recent ACA are some examples of policies that have attempted to strengthen the role of primary care within the US healthcare system. Some experts have suggested that the ACA and the aging population will place an increased burden on the primary care workforce in the USA, contributing to a severe workforce shortage in the future [71]. Although about one-third of practicing physicians work in primary care, less than a fourth of current medical school graduates are pursuing careers in primary care fields, and many primary care physicians are projected to retire in coming years, raising additional concerns that the future US primary care workforce will be unable to respond to the growing demand for primary care [72]. A factor contributing to the small percentage of graduating medical students that pursue residencies in primary care is the significantly lower salaries in these fields, a trend that has continued despite some efforts to reduce this disparity [71, 73].

Similarly, in order to incentivize providers to accept patients newly eligible for Medicaid under the reforms, the ACA temporarily raises reimbursement for PCPs serving Medicaid patients to the same level as Medicare reimbursements [74]. However, a study found that those states that have a low supply of PCPs serving Medicaid enrollees already have higher reimbursement levels [74]. Therefore, this increase may have little effect in increasing the supply of PCPs available to care for disadvantaged groups, such as the Medicaid population.

In order to address these fears, more research is needed on the capabilities and capacities of the current

PCP workforce, as well as projections about how it will change over time. Indeed, a 2011 Robert Wood Johnson Foundation (RWJF) report observes that workforce projections are complicated [66]. The report cautions that although the workforce is likely to be strained by the country's changing demographics and increasing demand under the ACA, other clinicians, such as NPs and PAs, in addition to new team-based models of care, may change primary care workforce needs in unanticipated ways [66]. Nevertheless, the irregular distribution of providers in the USA remains a significant issue that is likely to continue inhibiting access to primary care services among particular segments of the population and in certain geographic regions [66].

Next steps and future directions have been identified to strengthen the primary care infrastructure abroad and in the USA. To start, there has been increasing interest in exploring how primary care and public health might better coordinate in order to support population health improvement efforts [75, 76]. A review of literature on the coordination of primary care with public health suggests that combinatory efforts can lead to improvements in the management of chronic diseases, control of communicable diseases, and in maternal and child health [76]. In addition, there is need for additional clarification on the unique roles of primary care and public health and the ways in which these sectors can work together [77].

In the USA in particular, new models of delivering care through patient-centered medical homes (PCMHs) and accountable care organizations (ACOs) require team-based approaches to care with a heavy emphasis on primary care. As previously discussed, some experts suggest that the shift to these models for delivering care will require an increased supply of primary care providers [58] whereas others note that little is definitively known about how these models of care will impact provider productivity [66]. This renewed interest in improving primary care capacity has led to some recommended initiatives for enhancing the stature of primary care in the USA, including increasing Title VII funding to better support the education of primary care providers that agree to practice in underserved communities [69, 70]; addressing salary disparities between PCPs and specialists by changing Medicare's resource-based relative value scale to give more equal reimbursement, which also influences private insurance reimbursement rates [78]; exploring the role that other primary care providers, such as NPs and PAs, can play in reducing burdens on primary care physicians [66]. Additional research is obviously needed; topics that should be examined include the methods and tools for conducting research on primary care, clinical issues of relevance to the practice of primary care, primary care service delivery, health systems (including the social and political factors affecting primary care provision), and how to improve the education and training of primary care providers [54].

2.4. PRIMARY CARE AND HEALTH

Logically, primary care is seen as an important medical specialty and healthcare necessity because it is assumed to have a positive impact on health outcomes; the USA and most other countries believe that increasing the quality and quantity of primary care services will lead to better population health. A number of ecological studies have examined the relationship between primary care infrastructure and health outcomes internationally as well as in the USA [79–83] at various levels of geographic units. Studies conducted in industrialized countries, such as member nations of the Organization for Economic Cooperation and Development (OECD), do indicate that stronger primary care systems are generally associated with better population health outcomes including lower mortality rates, rates of premature death and hospitalizations for ambulatory care sensitive conditions, and higher infant birth weight, life expectancy, and satisfaction with the healthcare system [79, 80, 82, 86]. Studies in the USA have also indicated that greater primary care availability in a community is correlated with both better health outcomes [87] and a decrease in utilization of more expensive types of health services, such as hospitalizations and emergency department (ED) visits [88].

Experiences in the international context suggest that primary care-oriented healthcare delivery systems can produce better health outcomes in addition to counteracting, to some extent, the negative impact of poor economic conditions on health [57]. Reforms of healthcare systems to emphasize primary care generally are associated with improved health outcomes, including evidence from several countries in Latin America and Asia [83]. However, given that these reforms typically included multiple components, attributing change in population health to any one aspect of the reform is difficult [83]. Increasing primary care availability in low- and middle-income countries also correlates with improved health; however, many of these studies are limited to child and infant health outcomes [81]. Additionally, much of the research in this setting consists of observational studies rather than more rigorous research designs, and studies may also use different definitions of what constitutes a "primary care system" or "program" [81].

In a review of US primary care and its relationship with health outcomes, Starfield et al. note that there may be several mechanisms of primary care that explain this positive association with population health: (1) better access to health services; (2) improved quality of care; (3) emphasis on prevention; (4) the identification and early management of conditions; (5) the combined impact of many characteristics of solid primary care systems; (6) reduction in unnecessary specialist care [89, 90].

Primary care and health service use were also studied in the USA using an interactional analysis instrument to characterize patient-centered care in the primary care setting and examine its relationship with healthcare utilization [91]. A total of 509 adult patients at a university medical center were randomized into groups receiving care by family physicians or general internists. An adaptation of the Davis Observation Code was used to measure patient-centered practices; the main outcome measures of the study were the patients' use of medical services and accrued charges over one year. The results indicated that higher amounts of patient-centered care were related to a significantly decreased annual number of visits to specialty providers, less frequent hospitalizations, and fewer laboratory and diagnostic tests. Total medical charges for the year were also significantly reduced.

Another US study examined the relationship between physician-patient connectedness and measures of physician performance [51]. 155,590 patients who made one or more visits to a study practice from 2003 to 2005 in the Massachusetts General Hospital adult primary care network were identified, and a validated algorithm was used to connect patients to physicians or practices. Performance measures, including breast, cervical, and colorectal cancer screening in eligible patients, hemoglobin A1C measurement and control in patients with diabetes, and low-density lipoprotein cholesterol measurement and control in patients with diabetes and coronary artery disease, were used to examine clinical performance. The results indicated that physician-connected patients were significantly more likely than practice-connected patients to receive guideline-consistent care. Receipt of preventive care varied more by whether patients were more or less connected to a primary care physician than by race or ethnicity, which are often cited as major determinants of healthcare usage.

The role of primary care in referral was studied in a multicountry project in Europe and Australia [92]. The study compared weight loss achieved through standard treatment in primary care versus weight loss achieved after referral by the primary care team to a commercial provider in the community. In this parallel group, nonblinded, randomized controlled trial, 772 overweight, and obese adults were recruited by primary care practices in Australia, Germany, and the UK to receive either 12 months of standard care, as defined by national treatment guidelines or 12 months of free membership in a commercial program; analysis was by intention to treat amongst the population who completed the 12-month assessment. The results showed that the participants referred to community-based commercial providers lost more than twice as much weight over the year as compared to those who received standard care. These results indicate that referral to a commercial weight loss program that provides regular weighing, advice about diet and physical activity, motivation, and group support can offer a clinically useful early intervention for weight management in overweight and obese people and can be delivered on a large scale as well. However, it also demonstrates that primary care physicians and teams have limits in the scope and quality of interventions they can provide; in this case, the primary care team provided better care through the referral to an outside company than through the team-managed care seen as standard.

The impact of primary care outreach was tested in a Canadian study [93] using a randomized, controlled trial design to evaluate the impact of a provider-initiated primary care outreach intervention as compared with usual care among older adults at risk of functional decline. The sample was comprised of 719 patients enrolled with 35 family physicians in five primary care networks in Hamilton, Ontario, Canada. The 12-month intervention, provided by experienced home care nurses from 2004 to 2006, consisted of a comprehensive initial assessment using the Resident Assessment Instrument for home care, collaborative care planning with patients, their families, and family physicians, health promotion activities, and referral to community health and social support services. The primary outcome measures were quality adjusted life years (QALYs), use and costs of health and social services, functional status, self-rated health, and mortality. The results for the mean difference in QALYs, overall cost of prescription drugs and services, and changes over 12 months in functional status and self-rated health were not statistically significant. Therefore, the results of this study do not support adoption of this particular preventive primary care intervention for this target population of high-risk older adults.

Another study conducted in Pittsburgh, Pennsylvania, examined the role of nurses in primary care [94]. This study evaluated findings from a trial treatment for behavioral problems in 163 clinically referred children from six primary care offices in Pittsburgh. Participants were randomized to be treated in either the on-site, nurse-administered intervention (PONI) in primary care or enhanced usual care (EUC) characterized by on-site diagnostic assessment and facilitated referral to a local mental health provider. The main outcomes were measured by standardized rating scales. The results showed that children randomized to the PONI intervention were significantly more likely to access their assigned treatment, received more direct treatment, adjunctive services, and a longer duration of treatment, and had greater levels of sibling participation than children assigned to receive EUC. These findings indicate that a psychosocial intervention for behavioral problems delivered by nurses in a primary care setting is feasible, improves access to mental health services, and has some clinical efficacy. Options for enhancing clinical outcomes may include multifaceted collaborative care interventions in the pediatric practice.

The impact of primary care on chronic disease management is the subject of much research. For example, a USA-based study examined the impact of a multifaceted intervention on cholesterol management in primary care practices [95]. The study used a practice-based trial to test the hypothesis that a multifaceted intervention consisting of guideline dissemination enhanced by a computerized decision support system (CDSS) would improve primary care physician adherence to the Third Adult Treatment Panel (ATP III) guidelines and improve the management of cholesterol levels. A total of 61 primary care families and internal medicine practices in North Carolina enrolled in the trial; 29 received the Third Adult Treatment Panel (ATP III) intervention and 32 received an alternate intervention (JNC-7). The ATP III providers received a personal digital assistant providing the Framingham risk scores and ATP III-recommended treatment. They examined 5,057 baseline and 3,821 follow-up medical records. The study reports the positive effect on screening of lipid levels and appropriate management of lipid level test results and concludes that a multifactorial intervention, including personal digital assistant-based decision support, may improve primary care physician adherence to the ATP III guidelines.

In a US study that focused on diabetes disease management, researchers used a randomized, controlled trial to examine the relationships among patient characteristics, labor inputs, and improvement in glycosylated hemoglobin (A1C) level in a primary care-based diabetes disease management program (DDMP) [96]. A total of 217 patients with type 2 diabetes mellitus and poor glucose control were enrolled. The results showed that patients in the intervention group had significantly greater improvement in A1C level than the control group that received no additional disease management support. In multivariate analysis, no significant differences in A1C level improvement were observed when stratified by age, race/ethnicity, income, or insurance status, and no interaction effect was observed between any covariate and intervention status. Labor inputs were similar regardless of age, race/ethnicity, sex, or education and may reflect the nondiscriminatory nature of providing algorithm-based disease management care.

The role of primary care in preventive care has also been studied. In a study conducted in Spain on physical activity promotion by general practitioners, researchers sought to assess the effectiveness of a physical activity promotion program at 11 Spanish public primary care centers using 6-, 12-, and 24-month follow-up measurements [97]. They recruited 4,317 individuals (2,248 intervention and 2,069 control), and fifty-six general practitioners (GPs) were randomly assigned to intervention or standard care (control) groups. The primary outcome measure was the change in self-reported physical activity from baseline. The results indicated that general practitioners were effective at increasing the level of physical activity among their inactive patients during the initial six months of an intervention but the effect leveled off at 12 and 24 months. Only the subgroup of patients receiving repeat prescriptions of physical activity maintained gains over the long term.

Many people suffering from mental health issues also receive health services in a primary care setting [98]. In the USA, an evaluation of a Department of Veterans Affairs (VA) program establishing primary care clinics in underserved communities found that while these clinics did improve access to more general health services, without a specialty mental healthcare component, they did not effectively expand access to mental health services [99]. Research is mixed on whether psychotherapy and counseling in the primary care setting is cost-effective but it does suggest that patients may be more open to these strategies than to antidepressant prescriptions, and psychotherapy may be more effective in treating depression than counseling [98]. Research has found that while counseling in primary care is associated with short-term improvement and patient satisfaction, there is little evidence of its effectiveness, in comparison to usual care, in treating depression in the long run [100].

An overview of low- and middle-income countries found that 14 countries, including China, with compre-hensive primary care (defined as >80% skilled birth atten-dance rates) experienced health gains compared with countries with more selective primary care approaches. These health improvements seemed to "depend on progression to comprehensive primary care with a reli-able referral system linking to functioning facilities" [101, p. 958]. However, the study looked at countries as a whole and so could not account for within-country variation, and additionally, the study defined countries as having comprehensive primary care based only upon their skilled birth attendance rates, and other primary care attributes were not considered.

In the USA, a growing body of research has focused on the impact of primary care supply, infrastructure, and models of care on health outcomes. A review of studies assessing the relationship between supply of PCPs and various outcomes, such as all-cause and disease-specific mortality, life expectancy, low birth weight, and self-rated health, found correlations at the state, county, and MSA levels [84]. Research also indicates that local supply of PCPs per capita, using radii around zip codes to define service areas, is associated positively with patient receipt of preventive health services and that this local primary care availability mediates, to some extent, the impact of socioeconomic factors on the receipt of preventive care [102]. In addition, according to one study, Medicaid-enrolled children who have access to high quality, family-centered primary care have both lower nonurgent and urgent hospitalization rates [103].

However, methodological challenges exist in conducting research linking PCP supply to population health. When doing these analyses, the ratio of primary care to specialist physicians may be a more appropriate measure than just physician supply [85]. For example, while a correlation exists between the PCP supply and health outcomes, there is no association between specialist supply and health outcomes [89, 90]. Therefore, using a measure of physician supply per capita, without consideration of the balance of primary care and specialist physicians, may skew findings.

In response to this policy-relevant research, next steps have included proposals to increase the supply of primary care physicians in the USA. Findings suggest that increasing the supply of PCPs by just one unit per 10,000 physicians might improve health outcomes by 0.66% to as much as 10.8%, depending on the outcome considered [84].

Further research is needed on which models of care produce the best health outcomes. While past research has indicated team-based care produces better outcomes in some settings, few studies have examined the use of teams in primary care practice [104].

Other issues will also continue to affect the relationship between primary care and health. Many experts believe that primary care will have to change practice models to improve patient outcomes and physician job satisfaction, as demonstrated in many of the previously mentioned researches. However, others have also argued that in order to revitalize primary care in the USA, major system-level change is needed, especially in the way that primary care physicians are compensated relative to specialists [105]. [...]

2.6. PRIMARY CARE AND COST

One consequence of having many specialists is the possibility that specialist care has contributed to increasing the volume of intensive, expensive, and invasive medical services and therefore the costs of healthcare [138–144]. Higher surgeon supply has been found to increase the demand for initial contacts with surgeons [145]. Many now frequently performed operations, such as coronary artery bypass, hip replacement, carotid endarterectomy, arthroscopy, laparoscopy, and heart and liver transplantation, were little known and hardly ever performed 50 years ago. Today, they are both fairly common and expensive.

Technological developments also drive up healthcare costs [146]. Systematic comparison across industrialized countries shows that the USA has higher rates of coronary surgery, diagnostic imaging, neurosurgery, treatment for end-stage renal disease, and cancer chemotherapy than any other country [147, 148]. As the disease prevalence for these conditions is still relatively low, an excess of specialists in these areas may lead to the performance of unnecessary procedures. The Congressional Subcommittee on Oversight and Investigations estimated that nationwide there were

2.4 million unnecessary operations performed annually, resulting in a cost of $3.9 billion and 11,900 deaths [149, 150]. Overall, primary care services are less costly than specialty services because they are less technology-intensive.

An economic analysis was conducted in the UK to assess the cost-effectiveness of Quality and Outcomes Framework (QOF) payments, which is an attempt to improve the quality of primary care in the UK through the use of financial rewards [151]. The study used 2004/2005 data on the QOF performance of all English primary care practices. Cost-effectiveness evidence was collected for a subset of nine QOF indicators with direct thera-peutic impact. The authors found that the proportional changes required to make QOF payments cost-effective varied widely between the indicators. It showed that QOF incentive payments are likely to be a cost-effective use of resources for a high proportion of primary care practices, and incentive payments are likely to be a good value for the NHS.

Health policy experts suggest that systems, models, and providers oriented toward primary care may achieve lower healthcare costs, a top priority in the USA [52, 133]. The bulk of the evidence suggests that PCPs order fewer diagnostic tests and procedures than specialists, leading to lower costs. In addition, having a usual source of care (defined as a primary care function, not explicitly as a PCP) is correlated with lower use of healthcare resources and lower rates of nonurgent emergency department visits, thus also decreasing costs [152]. On a systems level, regions of the USA with a higher PCP to specialist ratio experience not only better health outcomes but also lower costs [152]. Comparative analyses have found that other countries with health systems oriented toward primary care, on average, also have lower costs and better population health outcomes [152].

In addition to these more macro-level demonstrations of relationships between the primary care system and healthcare spending, cost-effectiveness studies and other forms of cost analyses can inform efforts to strengthen and improve primary care delivery [153]. One area of research explores what settings produce the best value or the highest quality care for the lowest costs. The community health center (CHC) program delivers primary care for vulnerable populations in areas identified by the Department of Health and Human Services' Health Resource and Services Administration as medically underserved [67]. A review of the literature on CHCs indicates that these centers provide quality primary care at low cost to especially disadvantaged populations [154]. However, the authors note that few studies have used formal cost-effectiveness methods to compare the value of CHCs to the value achieved in other primary care settings [154]. One recent study using Medicaid claims data to compare CHCs to other primary care settings found that while hospital outpatient departments and CHCs have similar costs, private physician practices actually have somewhat lower costs [155].

Some suggest that certain models of care may also lower costs. Staub, for instance, has argued that larger primary care group practices can apply management and technology innovations more fluidly than smaller practices, lowering the costs associated with these kinds of changes [156]. Others have looked to the patient-centered medical home (PCMH) as one model that shows promise in reducing healthcare spending. While the literature to date generally supports an association between the improved access and coordination of the PCMH model and reduced hospitalizations and ED visits, other predicted effects, such as decreased use of unnecessary tests, procedures, and referrals, have not yet been demonstrated [157]. One example of an integrated program, the Geisinger Health System's Proven Health Navigator (PHN), has led to cost savings of 4.3% to 7.1% [158]. The program's success in reducing costs may be an inspiration to other integrated delivery systems or primary care practices seeking to adopt the PCMH model [158]. Friedman et al. also observe that health professionals who are not PCPs can perform primary care functions, an important consideration for the team-oriented PCMH model. Research suggests that care by nonphysicians, like physician assistants (PAs), for example, may be less costly than care by physicians [159].

Access to care may also impact costs. One study assessed a low-cost primary care physician access program's impact on ED use, noting that while the increased access may have prompted patients to change where they sought care for nonurgent purposes, the study could not demonstrate statistically significant cost savings [109]. This study and the evaluation of the Geisinger PCMH suggest that primary care interventions may require long periods of time to demonstrate financial savings [109, 158]. An eight-year study assessing the impact of a primary care case management (PCCM) program in Iowa's Medicaid program did demonstrate reductions in costs due to shifting expenses from the hospital to outpatient setting. These savings increased over time, reinforcing what other studies suggest: these desired significant cost savings may take time to achieve [160]. Chernew et al. explored how PCP/specialist supply influences cost, and the findings indicated that increasing the PCP supply may accrue a short-term advantage but does not address long-term problems. Although the proportion of the workforce comprised of PCPs in contrast to specialists likely affects healthcare expenditures, balancing the workforce in favor of PCPs may do little to curb the rate of growth in healthcare spending and thus will not reduce overall costs [161].

PCCM programs, like the one implemented for the Iowa Medicaid program, use the gatekeeper approach, in which patients select a PCP and are then required to obtain referrals through this PCP to see specialists, reducing unnecessary specialist appointments and procedures and therefore reducing healthcare costs. The PCP also may coordinate care for a panel of patients in a cost-effective manner [160].

Another intervention that has been touted as a potential way to reduce the costs of medical care in the USA is health IT. Research indicates that health IT systems may yield financial gains for PCPs by reducing drug expenditures, reducing utilization of expensive tests in favor of other equally useful diagnostic methods, and decreasing billing mistakes [162]. One study of the implementation of an electronic medical record (EMR) system in primary care clinics found cost savings that increased over time [162].

Other lines of research explore the cost-effectiveness of particular interventions conducted in the primary care setting [42, 98, 100, 163, 164]. For example, studies have explored the cost-effectiveness of different techniques designed to increase cancer screenings [42, 163], diabetes self-management programs [164], mental health interventions [98, 100], smoking cessation treatment, and life-style counseling and interventions [166], all within the primary care setting. This type of research seeks to inform quality improvement efforts in primary care with cost-effectiveness information. Ideally, PCPs could use this information to provide both higher quality and more efficient care.

2.7. PRIMARY CARE AND EQUITY

Better primary care is also associated with more equitable distribution of health within a population [89, 90, 167, 168]. The annual National Healthcare Disparities Report in the USA [169] stated that equitable primary care eliminates disparities "related to preventive services and management of common chronic diseases typically delivered in primary care settings" [170]. Primary care providers deliver a disproportionate share of ambulatory care to disadvantaged populations. Improved access to primary care was associated with reduced mortality rates, better health outcomes, and lower costs [6, 171–175]. A higher proportion of PCPs in a given area has also been shown to lead to lower spending on healthcare [161]. Additionally, an increase of one primary care physician per a population of 10,000 is associated with a reduction of 1.44 deaths, a 2.5% reduction in infant mortality, and a 3.2% reduction of low birthweight on average in the population [167, 168, 176–179]. Such associations hold even in the presence of income inequality and other health determinants [172–175]. Adults who have PCPs as their regular source of care experience lower mortality and incur reduced healthcare costs [6].

Research has also shown that primary care may play an important role in mitigating the adverse health effects of income inequality [180–183]. Specifically, research has demonstrated associations between income inequality and self-rated health and primary care and self-rated health [181]. Therefore, the pathway through which income inequality impacts health may be partly attenuated by primary care [182]. Access to quality primary care may have the largest impact on health in areas with the highest levels of income inequality [182]. However, socioeconomic status may also reduce to some extent the impact of primary care on health [182]. The relationship between race, income inequality, primary care availability, and health is complicated; in stratified analyses of the impacts of primary care and income inequality on mortality, Shi and Starfield [183] found while independent associations between primary care and mortality and income inequality and mortality persisted after controlling for other socioeconomic variables among white Americans, the relationship between primary care physician supply and mortality lost its statistical significance with the inclusion of other socioeconomic factors in the model.

Primary care availability may also be more strongly correlated with health outcomes in areas with greater levels of income inequality, suggesting that expanding primary care availability in these areas may have a substantial impact on population health [180]. However, only certain specialties under the umbrella of primary care may have this impact. For example, family medicine has been found to have the strongest inverse relationship with mortality [172–175]. These findings have been consistent in examinations of mortality at the state level [172–175], at the county level [167, 168], in comparisons of urban and nonurban areas [167, 168], and in stratifications by race [167, 168].

In the USA, racial and ethnic minorities face greater difficulty accessing regular primary care than white Americans and use hospitals more often than private clinics as usual sources of care [184]. Challenges included long wait times and difficulty obtaining timely appointments. Addressing these barriers and ensuring more equitable access to high quality primary care may translate into reduced disparities in self-rated health status [176–178].

Access to primary care may have the greatest impact on health status for racial and ethnic minorities living in poverty [176–178]. However, research exploring why racial and ethnic minorities in the USA receive fewer preventive services determined that while frequency of visits to primary care physicians likely explains a small portion of the disparity, factors related to poverty are significantly more important [185]. While some research has suggested that physician-patient racial concordance may positively affect the quality of care racial/ethnic minority patients receive, other research has not borne out these conclusions [186].

A US study looking at the Latino population aimed to identify subgroup variations in having a patient-centered medical home, the PCMH's impact on disparities, and factors associated with Latinos having a PCMH in the USA [187]. The 2005 Medical Expenditure Panel Survey (MEPS) Household Component that sampled 24,000 adults, including 6,200 Latinos, was used in this analysis. Self-reports of preventive care and patient experiences were also examined. The results showed that white (57.1%) and Puerto Rican (59.3%) adults were most likely to have a PCMH, while Mexican/Mexican Americans (35.4%) and Central and South Americans (34.2%)

were least likely. Much of this disparity was caused by lack of access to a regular provider. Respondents with a PCMH had higher rates of preventive care and positive patient experiences. Disparities in care were eliminated or reduced for Latinos with PCMHs. The regression models showed that private insurance, which is less common among Latinos than whites, was an important predictor of having a PCMH. These findings indicate that eliminating healthcare disparities will require assuring access to a PCMH and that addressing differences in healthcare coverage that contribute to lower rates of Latino access to the PCMH will also reduce disparities.

As seen in the previous study, insurance status is associated with access to primary care and the quality of that care [30]. The uninsured have greater difficulty accessing good primary care than the insured; among the insured, those with private insurance have better access to quality primary care than the publicly insured [30]. Those with health maintenance organization (HMO) plans have more comprehensive care but poorer measures of longitudinal and coordinated care than those in fee for service (FFS) plans [30].

Children also experience racial and ethnic disparities in access to and quality of primary care [188]. Stevens and Shi propose the following research agenda to explore health disparities in children further: (1) conduct research using more racial and ethnic granularity rather than categorizing groups superficially; (2) explore the role of language in contributing to health disparities; (3) consider cultural influences; (4) examine how health systems-level policies and factors contribute to disparities [188]. Recent attention has focused on how models, such as the patient-centered medical home, may improve quality of care for children. Yet research on the association between race and ethnicity and having a medical home has determined that minority children have lower odds of having healthcare experiences that contain features of the medical home, such as having a usual provider, a provider who spends sufficient time with him or her, and a provider who communicates well [189].

One unique population on which there is little literature is the migrant worker population. Part of the reason for this gap in research is the difficulty in determining how many migrant workers are living currently in the USA [190]. Although the federally qualified health center (FQHC) program currently provides primary care to an estimated 20% of agricultural workers, most migrant workers face significant structural barriers to accessing adequate primary healthcare [190].

The Patient Protection and Affordable Care Act may impact disparities in access to and quality of primary care by expanding insurance coverage and funding for FQHCs and the National Health Service Corps, which repays loans to physicians and health professionals practicing in shortage areas [191]. In addition, it includes innovations like the community-based collaborative care networks, which support low-income populations in accessing medical homes [191]. [...]

2.9. PRIMARY CARE AND HEALTHCARE REFORM

A number of industrialized countries have embarked on healthcare reforms aimed, at least in part, at strengthening their primary care delivery systems. For example, a primary care reform in Quebec, Canada, was studied to see if/how patients' perceptions of the quality of care changed [210]. The study used a before-and-after comparison of the perceptions of patients to evaluate how primary care reform affected patients' experiences in primary care. A random sample of 1,046 participants from five family medicine groups (FMGs) in two regions of Quebec completed both the baseline and follow-up questionnaires. The authors found that perceptions of relational and informational continuity increased significantly, whereas organizational and first-contact accessibility and service responsiveness did not change significantly. Perception of physician-nurse coordination remained unchanged, but perception of primary care physician-specialist coordination decreased significantly. The proportion of participants reporting visits with nurses and reporting use of FMGs' emergency services increased significantly from baseline to followup. The findings showed that the reorganization of primary care services resulted in considerable changes in care practices, leading to improvements in patients' continuity of care but not to improvements in accessibility of care.

Another recent study assessed changes in patient experiences of primary care during health service reforms in England between 2003 and 2007 [211]. The researchers conducted a cross-sectional study of family practices in which questionnaires were sent to serial samples of patients in 42 representative general practices in England. Up to 12 patients with a confirmed diagnosis of each chronic illness (coronary heart disease, diabetes, or asthma) were randomly sampled in each practice. In addition, a random sample of 200 adult patients (excluding patients who reported any long-term condition) in each practice were also mailed a questionnaire. The results show that were no significant changes in quality of care reported by either group of patients between 2003 and 2007 regarding communication, nursing care, coordination, and overall satisfaction. Some aspects of access improved significantly for patients with chronic disease, but not for the patients without a long-term condition. The findings indicate that there were modest improvements in access to care for patients with chronic illness, but overall, patients now find it somewhat harder to obtain care, affecting care continuity. This outcome may be related to incorrect incentives to provide rapid appointments or to the increased number of specialized clinics in primary care. This research indicates that the possibility of unintended effects needs to be considered when introducing pay for performance schemes.

The impact of China's New Rural Cooperative Medical Scheme (NCMS) and its implications for rural primary healthcare were evaluated in a study that performed a difference-in-difference analysis to determine whether China's NCMS has corrected distortions in rural primary care and whether the policy has affected the operation and use of village health clinics [212]. A total of 160 village primary care clinics and 8,339 individuals within 25 rural counties across five Chinese provinces were involved in this study. The study sought to evaluate the effect of NCMS by using individual level and village clinic level data collected in 2004 (shortly after the introduction of the scheme in selected regions) and in 2007 (after the dramatic expansion of the scheme across most rural areas). For individuals, NCMS is not clearly related to the use of medical care, but it may have redirected patients away from specialized facilities to village clinics. On the clinic level, NCMS has increased clinics' weekly patient flow and gross income, but not annual net revenue. Increases in patient flow and gross, but not net, clinic income may reflect desirable reductions in the provision of specialized, high profit services and rates of drug sales.

3. CONCLUSION

Primary care is imperative for building a strong healthcare system that ensures positive health outcomes, effectiveness and efficiency, and health equity. It is the first contact in a healthcare system for individuals and is characterized by longitudinality, comprehensiveness, and coordination. It provides individual and family-focused and community-oriented care for preventing, curing or alleviating common illnesses and disabilities, and promoting health.

Many countries in the world have embraced primary care, using a variety of structures and models. Lessons from these countries could serve as case studies for the US healthcare system, which currently faces an imbalance between specialty and primary care as well as a significant shortage and inequitable distribution in the primary care workforce. Different types of indicators and tools have been developed to measure the function of primary care, the performance of providers and facilities, quality of care, and so forth, but the need for more indicators and more data continues. Patient-centered measurements are gradually replacing disease specific measurements to yield more accurate assessment of primary care.

In both developed and developing countries, primary care has been demonstrated to be associated with enhanced access to healthcare services, better health outcomes, and a decrease in hospitalization and use of emergency department visits. Primary care can also help counteract the negative impact of poor economic conditions on health. Therefore, research suggests the need to increase the supply of primary care physicians in the USA. Further research is also needed to evaluate what models of primary care can produce the best health outcomes.

There are many factors determining quality of care, such as ease of access (including availability of after-hours care, length of office wait time, travel time to an appointment, and flexibility in selecting a PCP), clinical quality, interpersonal aspects, continuity, structure through which primary care is delivered, and insurance coverage. Although studies in international settings have compared quality of care in primary care and specialty care settings, the results were mixed, and further research is needed to elucidate how system-level factors, and certain policies may influence quality in the USA.

In addition, research has indicated that countries and regions more oriented to primary care have lower healthcare costs but better health outcomes, although further studies using formal cost-effectiveness methods need to be conducted. Cost-effectiveness of primary care has been tentatively established through a few interventions conducted in primary care settings, and adoption of health information systems in primary care settings may further yield financial gains.

Furthermore, better primary care is correlated with more equitable distribution of health within a population and can mitigate the adverse effects of income inequality, which is especially important in the USA where racial and ethnic minorities face greater difficulties accessing regular primary care. This in turn emphasizes the significant role of CHCs in the USA in providing primary care services to vulnerable groups and reducing disparities. CHCs in the USA are primary care facilities that provide family-oriented services to meet the healthcare needs of medically underserved populations. However, difficulties in recruiting primary care providers and maintaining financial viability are major challenges to the sustainability of CHCs, which subsequently influences primary care services available to and health outcomes for these underserved populations. Additionally, research on health disparities in children and migrant workers is still lacking and needs further attention.

Lastly, healthcare reforms aimed at strengthening the primary care system have been implemented in a number of countries, both developed and developing, and have generally proven to improve the healthcare system as a whole. The Patient Protection and Affordable Care Act (ACA) also emphasizes primary care in the USA. Future assessments focusing on the impact of the ACA on primary care, health outcomes, healthcare costs, and health disparities should be conducted to serve as an empirical basis for policy making in the future.

1. Based on this paper, how would you characterize access to primary care services in the United States?

2. What are the benefits of primary care for health care systems overall?

"WHY THE US DOES NOT HAVE UNIVERSAL HEALTH CARE, WHILE MANY OTHER COUNTRIES DO," BY TIMOTHY CALLAGHAN, FROM *THE CONVERSATION*, MAY 14, 2017

The lead-up to the House passage of the American Health Care Act (AHCA) on May 4, which passed by a narrow majority after a failed first attempt, provided a glimpse into just how difficult it is to gain consensus on health care coverage.

In the aftermath of the House vote, many people have asked: Why are politicians struggling to find consensus on the AHCA instead of pursuing universal coverage? After all, most advanced industrialized countries have universal health care.

As a health policy and politics scholar, I have some ideas. Research from political science and health services points to three explanations.

NO. 1: AMERICAN CULTURE IS UNIQUE

One key reason is the unique political culture in America. As a nation that began on the back of immigrants with an entrepreneurial spirit and without a feudal system to ingrain a rigid social structure, Americans are more likely to be individualistic.

In other words, Americans, and conservatives in particular, have a strong belief in classical liberalism and the idea that the government should play a limited role in society. Given that universal coverage inherently clashes with this belief in individualism and limited government, it is perhaps not surprising that it has never been enacted in America even as it has been enacted elsewhere.

Public opinion certainly supports this idea. Survey research conducted by the International Social Survey Program has found that a lower percentage of Americans believe health care for the sick is a government responsibility than individuals in other advanced countries like Canada, the U.K., Germany or Sweden.

NO. 2: INTEREST GROUPS DON'T WANT IT

Even as American political culture helps to explain the health care debate in America, culture is far from the only reason America lacks universal coverage. Another factor that has limited debate about national health insurance is the role of interest groups in influencing the political process. The legislative battle over the content of the ACA, for example, generated US$1.2 billion in lobbying in 2009 alone.

The insurance industry was a key player in this process, spending over $100 million to help shape the ACA and keep private insurers, as opposed to the government, as the key cog in American health care.

While recent reports suggest strong opposition from interest groups to the AHCA, it is worth noting that even when confronted with a bill that many organized interests view as bad policy, universal health care has not been brought up as an alternative.

NO. 3: ENTITLEMENT PROGRAMS ARE HARD IN GENERAL TO ENACT

A third reason America lacks universal health coverage and that House Republicans struggled to pass their plan even in a very conservative House chamber is that America's political institutions make it difficult for massive entitlement programs to be enacted. As policy experts have pointed out in studies of the U.S. health system, the country doesn't "have a comprehensive national health insurance system because American political institutions are structurally biased against this kind of comprehensive reform."

The political system is prone to inertia, and any attempt at comprehensive reform must pass through the obstacle course of congressional committees, budget estimates, conference committees, amendments and a potential veto while opponents of reform publicly bash the bill.

BOTTOM LINE: UNIVERSAL COVERAGE UNLIKELY TO HAPPEN

Ultimately, the United States remains one of the only advanced industrialized nations without a comprehensive national health insurance system and with little prospect for one developing under President Trump or even subsequent presidents because of the many ways America is exceptional.

Its culture is unusually individualistic, favoring personal over government responsibility; lobbyists are particularly active, spending billions to ensure that private insurers maintain their status in the health system; and our institutions are designed in a manner that limits major social policy changes from happening.

As long as the reasons above remain, there is little reason to expect universal coverage in America anytime soon.

1. Why does the author feel universal health care is not a good fit for the United States?

2. Does the author feel anything could change in the conditions of the US that might allow for universal health care?

CHAPTER 2

WHAT THE GOVERNMENT AND POLITICIANS SAY

Health care has been a source of ongoing political discussion for much of the last century, as lawmakers and leaders try to find ways to ensure access to care for vulnerable populations. But lawmakers have struggled to agree on what an ideal solution might look like, and that divergence has only grown in the past decade. Democrats celebrated the passage of the Affordable Care Act in 2012, which aimed to expand access to health care and lower costs, while Republicans criticized it for requiring people to have insurance and for burdening small businesses. But no consensus has yet been made, and politicians continue to argue for either greater deregulation or expanded access to government programs.

"KEY FACTS ON THE 'REPEAL AND REPLACE' HEALTH CARE BILL," BY GOVTRACK INSIDER, FROM GOVTRACK.US AT *MEDIUM*, MARCH 9, 2017

The American Health Care Act of 2017 (AHCA), H.R. 1628, is the House Republicans' leading proposal to "repeal and replace" the Affordable Care Act (aka Obamacare, but we'll abbreviate it ACA) and "defund" Planned Parenthood. Revealed to the public on March 6 as a draft at readthebill. gop and then formally introduced as a bill in Congress on March 20 (more on that at the end), the bill may be voted on by both chambers before the end of the month.

Update 1—March 20:

Since publishing this article on on March 9, minor changes to the AHCA proposal were revealed on March 14 and then substantive changes were proposed on March 20 when the proposal was formally introduced as a bill in Congress. The basic framework of the legislation outlined below remains essentially the same.

Update 2—May 4:

A new deal among the Republican factions was reached. The changes to the AHCA, as reported by the Rules committee, are:

- States may opt-out of providing the ACA's essential health benefits.
- States may opt-out of requiring premiums to be the same for all people of the same age, so while individuals with pre-existing conditions must be offered health insurance there is no limit on the cost of that insurance.

A new $8 billion fund would help lower premiums for these individuals.

- States may opt-out of limiting premium differences based on age.
- There would be a new $15 billion fund for risk sharing to help states lower premiums.

WHAT'S STAYING THE SAME

The bill would keep intact much of the ACA. In fact, it wouldn't formally repeal any significant parts of the ACA.

As the Republican website readthebill.gop explains, the AHCA would "preserve vital patient protections" created by the ACA:

- *The AHCA would still "prohibit health insurers from denying coverage or charging more money to patients based on pre-existing conditions." UPDATE—This is no longer the case, see the top of the article.*
- The AHCA would keep the ACA's requirement that dependents can stay "on their parents' plan **until they are 26.**"
- The **exchanges (aka marketplaces)** run by the federal government and states, which listed individual and small business health insurance plans, would continue as under the ACA.
- The AHCA would also **continue to provide subsidies** for premiums that are based on income, although the formula would be completely different and the subsidy would likely be much less for young, low-income Americans.

And according to this summary from USA Today:

- The AHCA would **keep some Medicaid benefits** for those that enroll prior to 2020 (more on that below).
- *The AHCA would keep the requirement that health plans cover essential benefits—but not for those on Medicaid. UPDATE—This is no longer the case, see the top of the article.*
- The AHCA would **keep the restriction that subsidies can't pay for health insurance that covers abortion**.

THE INDIVIDUAL MANDATE STAYS TOO, BUT BY ANY OTHER NAME

The AHCA even includes a penalty for individuals who don't get coverage, referred to as the "individual mandate" in the ACA. While the ACA imposes a roughly $700 per year penalty for not holding health insurance, the AHCA would instead impose a surcharge of up to 30% the next time you get insurance after a lapse in coverage.

Depending on your premiums and how long you go without insurance, the ACHA's penalty could be more or less than the ACA's current penalty. In many cases, it might be about the same.

WHAT'S BEING EXPANDED

- Contribution limits to **Health Savings Accounts (HSAs)** would be increased to encourage their use. With HSAs, you can put aside some of your income for medical expenses and not pay taxes on it. (More on that here.)
- Under the AHCA, federal subsidies for paying premiums could be used to pay for insurance both from and not from the exchanges.

WHAT'S GOING AWAY

Some parts of the ACA would end:

IF YOU'RE ON MEDICAID...

- The ACA expanded **Medicaid eligibility** in 32 states that opted in to it. The AHCA would reverse the eligibility expansion beginning in 2020 (anyone enrolled by then would remain enrolled), and it would reduce federal support for Medicaid with caps on coverage.
- The ACA expanded required benefits **under Medicaid, such as mental health and addiction services**, which would no longer be required.

IF YOU'RE COVERED THROUGH YOUR EMPLOYER...

- Fines would be eliminated for **large employers** that don't provide health plans.
- **Small-business tax credits** would end in 2020.

IF YOU'RE ON AN INDIVIDUAL PLAN...

- The ACA limited what health insurance providers could charge in premiums. Under the AHCA, those limits would be adjusted so that younger people might see lower premiums and older people much higher premiums. *UPDATE—See the May 4 update at the top of the article.*
- The ACA's complex **cost-sharing provisions** that lowered costs for some low-income Americans would be eliminated.
- The ACA's awkward bronze/silver/platinum levels would go away.

OTHER CHANGES...

- A long list of taxes created by the ACA to pay for its subsidies would be eliminated, but some new taxes will be added, such as a new tax on the value of health insurance provided by an employer.
- Parts of last year's last-minute bipartisan 21st Century Cures Act would be defunded.

"DEFUNDING" PLANNED PARENTHOOD

The AHCA would also prohibit federal funding from going to Planned Parenthood, mostly through Medicaid, for one year.

This would pause federal reimbursements for Planned Parenthood's reproductive health, maternal health, and child health services—but not its abortion services because federal funds are already prohibited from being used for abortion.

WHAT'S THE BOTTOM LINE?

How the AHCA would affect you depends on your income, how you get your health insurance, and what kinds of health care you need.

- For older, low-income Americans with health insurance from the individual market: Premiums could increase by $3,600 for a 55-year-old earning $25,000 a year and $8,400 for a 64-year-old earning $15,000 a year. [AARP]
- For low-income Americans covered by **Medicaid**, the federal cap on support would likely lead to fewer benefits and higher out-of-pocket costs. [AARP] 5–18 million individuals are predicted to lose Medicaid coverage entirely. [NYTimes]

- If you are covered **through your employer**, your employer would be allowed to stop providing coverage—and that's made more likely because tax credits and the tax advantage for employer-provided coverage would be eliminated. But experts are split on whether the AHCA will affect employer coverage—and even whether the ACA ever had any effect on employer coverage to begin with. [NYTimes]
- Americans with **income around $40,000-$75,000** who purchase an individual plan may be better off because the ACA's subsidies for low-income Americans would be spread out to income up to $75,000. [USA Today] (Unless premiums go up too.) If **your income is below that**, some of your subsidies are now going to go to other people with higher income.
- If you have **an income of $200,000 or more**, or investment income, you can expect your tax bill to go down—those making $1 million or more can expect around $50,000 less in taxes each year.

Major changes to the health insurance market like the ACA and AHCA have far-reaching effects on federal spending and the economy. But experts polled by *The New York Times* are split on whether the AHCA will save the government or cost more because the AHCA lowers both government spending and tax revenue.

ODDS OF PASSAGE

Despite now controlling both the legislative and executive branches, and having previously voted successfully 45 times in the House to repeal the ACA, the Republicans' AHCA is not a done deal.

On the one hand, both the House Energy & Commerce and Ways and Means Committees passed their respective sections of legislation on March 9 with party line votes. On the other hand, the House Freedom Caucus, some high profile senators like Mike Lee (R-UT) and Rand Paul (R-KY), and industry groups like the American Medical Association and American Hospital Association have all spoken publicly against the legislation—some for the reason that it does not repeal *enough* of Obamacare. No Democrats will likely support it. The ACA also has all-time high support from the American public, with support reaching 54 percent last month.

USAGE OF THE BUDGET RECONCILIATION PROCESS

The Republicans don't have the votes to pass the AHCA the normal way. Knowing that it would be filibustered by Senate Democrats, Republicans are using the "budget reconciliation" process to move their bill forward. Budget reconciliation makes one bill each year immune to a filibuster, and the AHCA is this year's bill. The Democrats used budget reconciliation to enact parts of the ACA originally, so the use of reconciliation to modify the ACA (but not repeal it) is fitting.

Reconciliation can only be used on some types of bills that affect the federal budget, limiting the sorts of provisions that can be included in the AHCA—a full repeal of the ACA wouldn't be permitted under reconciliation rules. The reconciliation process also requires the House Budget committee to formally introduce the bill *after* it goes through committee—that's why the AHCA is a draft and not yet a bill and why it does not yet appear on GovTrack.us.

Although there are procedural similarities between how the ACA was enacted and what is happening now with the AHCA, there are also significant differences. The ACA was enacted after vigorous debate on competing and substantive policy proposals for nearly a year, with most of the final text available for several months before it was signed by President Obama. The AHCA is on track to going from draft to law within a matter of weeks and with hearings occurring when America is asleep.

1. How would the ACHA have altered the ACA?

2. Based on this article, what role do tax subsidies and credits play in health care access?

"REMARKS BY THE PRESIDENT ON THE AFFORDABLE CARE ACT," FROM THE OBAMA WHITE HOUSE ARCHIVES, OCTOBER 20, 2016

THE PRESIDENT: Hello, Miami! (Applause.) Thank you so much. Well, everybody have a seat. Have a seat. It is good to see all of you! It's good to be back at Miami-Dade! (Applause.) One of my favorite institutions! (Applause.) Love this school.

I want to thank your longtime president and great friend, Eduardo J. Padrón. (Applause.) And to all the faculty and staff, and of course, most importantly, the students, for hosting me -- I want to say how grateful I am. I want to thank the wonderful elected officials who are here today. I'm going to just point out two outstanding members of Congress -- Debbie Wasserman Schultz -- (applause) -- and Ted Deutch. (Applause.)

So this is one of my last visits here as President. Now, once I'm not President --

AUDIENCE MEMBER: Nooo --

THE PRESIDENT: No, no, the good news is, once I'm no longer President I can come more often. (Applause.) Right now, usually I can only come to Florida when I'm working. But when I'm out of office, I can come here for fun. (Laughter.)

But the first thing I want to say is thank you for your support, and thank you for the opportunity and the privilege you've given me to serve these past eight years. I remember standing just a few blocks north of here in the closing days of the 2008 campaign. And at that point, we were already realizing that we were in the midst of the worst economic crisis of our lifetimes. We didn't know where the bottom would be. We were still in the middle of two wars. Over 150,000 of our troops were overseas. But thanks to the hard work and the determination of the American people, when I come here today the story is different.

Working together, we've cut the unemployment rate in Florida by more than half. Across the country, we turned years of job losses into the longest streak of job creation on record. We slashed our dependence on foreign oil, doubled our production of renewable energy. Incomes are rising again -- they rose more last year than any time ever recorded. Poverty is falling -- fell more last year than any time since 1968. Our graduation rates from high school are at record highs. College enrollment is significantly higher than it was when we came into office. Marriage equality is a reality in all 50 states. (Applause.)

So we've been busy. This is why I've got gray hair. (Laughter.) But we did one other thing. We fought to make sure that in America, health care is not just a privilege, but a right for every single American. And that's what I want to talk about today. (Applause.) That's what I want to talk about here today.

You've heard a lot about Obamacare, as it's come to be known. You heard a lot about it in the six and a half years since I signed it into law. And some of the things you heard might even be true. But one thing I want to start with is just reminding people why it is that we fought for health reform in the first place. Because it was one of the key motivators in my campaign.

And it wasn't just because rising health costs were eating into workers' paychecks and straining budgets for businesses and for governments. It wasn't just because, before the law was passed, insurance companies could just drop your coverage because you got sick, right at the time you needed insurance most.

It was because of you. It was because of the stories that I was hearing all around the country, and right here in Florida -- hearing from people who had been forced to fight a broken health care system at the same time as they were fighting to get well.

It was about children like Zoe Lihn, who needed heart surgery when she was just 15 hours old -- just a baby, just a infant. And she was halfway to hitting her lifetime insurance cap before she was old enough to walk. Her parents had no idea how they could possibly make sure that she continued to make progress. And today, because of the Affordable Care Act, Zoe is in first grade and she's loving martial arts. And she's got a bright future ahead of her. (Applause.)

We fought so hard for health reform because of women like Amanda Heidel, who lives here in South Florida. As a girl, she was diagnosed with diabetes -- and that's a disease with costs that can add up quickly if you don't have insurance, can eat away at your dreams. But thanks to the Affordable Care Act, Amanda got to stay on her parents' plan after college. When she turned 26, Amanda went online, she shopped for an affordable health insurance plan that covered her medications. Today, she's pursuing a doctorate in psychology. And Amanda said that the Affordable Care Act "has given me the security and freedom to choose how I live my life." The freedom and security to choose how I live my life. That's what this was all about.

Zoe and Amanda, the people who I get letters from every single day describing what it meant not to fear that if they got sick, or a member of their family got sick, if they, heaven forbid, were in an accident, that somehow they could lose everything.

So because of this law, because of Obamacare, another 20 million Americans now know the financial security of health insurance. So do another 3 million children, thanks in large part to the Affordable Care Act and the improvements, the enhancements that we made to the Children's Health Insurance Program. And the net result is that never in American history has the uninsured rate been lower than it is today. Never. (Applause.) And that's true across the board. It's dropped among women. It's dropped among Latinos and African Americans, every other demographic group. It's worked.

Now, that doesn't mean that it's perfect. No law is. And it's true that a lot of the noise around the health care debate, ever since we tried to pass this law, has been nothing more than politics. But we've also always known -- and I have always said -- that for all the good that the Affordable Care Act is doing right now -- for as big a step forward as it was -- it's still just a first step. It's like building a starter home -- or buying a starter home. It's a lot better than not having a home, but you hope that over time you make some improvements.

And in fact, since we first signed the law, we've already taken a number of steps to improve it. And we can do even more -- but only if we put aside all the politics rhetoric, all the partisanship, and just be honest about what's working, what needs fixing and how we fix it.

So that's what I want to do today. This isn't kind of a rah-rah speech. I might get into the details. I hope you don't mind. (Laughter.)

So let's start with a basic fact. The majority of Americans do not -- let me repeat -- do not get health care through the Affordable Care Act. Eighty percent or so of Americans get health care on the job, through their employer, or they get health care through Medicaid, or they get health care through Medicare. And so for most Americans, the Affordable Care Act, Obama, has not affected your coverage -- except to make it stronger.

Because of the law, you now have free preventive care. Insurance companies have to offer that in whatever policy they sell. Because of the law, you now have free checkups for women. Because of the law, you get free mammograms. (Applause.) Because of the law, it is harder for insurance companies to discriminate against you because you're a woman when you get health insurance. (Applause.) Because of the law, doctors are finding better ways to perform heart surgeries and delivering healthier babies, and treating chronic disease, and reducing the number of people that, once they're in the hospital, end up having to return to the hospital.

So you're getting better quality even though you don't know that Obamacare is doing it.

AUDIENCE MEMBER: Thanks, Obama.

THE PRESIDENT: Thanks, Obama. (Laughter and applause.)

Because of the law, your annual out-of-pocket spending is capped. Seniors get discounts on their prescription drugs because of the law. Young people can stay on their parents' plan -- just like Amanda did -- because of the law. (Applause.) And Amanda was able to stay on her parents' plan and then get insurance after she aged out, even though she has what used to be called a preexisting condition -- because we made it illegal to discriminate against people with preexisting conditions. (Applause.)

By the way, before this law, before Obamacare, health insurance rates for everybody -- whether you got your insurance on the job, or you were buying it on your own -- health insurance rates generally were going up really fast. This law has actually slowed down the pace of health care inflation. So, every year premiums have gone up, but they've gone up the slowest in 50 years since Obamacare was passed. In fact, if your family gets insurance through your job, your family is paying, on average, about $3,600 less per year than you would be if the cost trends that had existed before the law were passed had continued. Think about that. That's money in your pocket.

Now, some people may say, well, I've seen my copays go up, or my networks have changed. But these are decisions that are made by your employers. It's not because of Obamacare. They're not determined by the Affordable Care Act.

So if the Affordable Care Act, if Obamacare hasn't changed the coverage of the 80 percent of Americans who already had insurance, except to make it a better value, except to make it more reliable, how has the law impacted the other 15 or 20 percent of Americans who didn't have health insurance through their job, or didn't qualify for Medicaid, or didn't qualify for Medicare?

Well, before the Affordable Care Act, frankly, you were probably out of luck. Either you had to buy health insurance on your own, because you weren't getting it through the job, and it was wildly expensive, and your premiums were going up all the time, and if you happened to get sick and use the insurance, the insurer the next year could drop you. And if you had had an illness like cancer or diabetes, or some other chronic disease, you couldn't buy new insurance because the insurance company's attitude was, you know what, this is just going to cost us money, we don't want to insure you.

So if you were trying to buy health insurance on your own, it was either hugely expensive or didn't provide very effective coverage. You might buy a policy thinking that it was going to cover you. It was sort of like when I was young and I bought my first car, I had to buy car insurance. And I won't name the insurance company, but I bought the insurance because it was the law, and I got the cheapest one I could get, because I didn't have any money -- and it was a really beat-up car. (Laughter.) And

I remember somebody rear-ends me, and I call up the insurance company, thinking maybe I can get some help, and they laughed at me. They're all like, what, are you kidding? (Laughter.) It didn't provide any coverage other than essentially allowing me to drive. (Laughter.)

Well, that's what it was like for a lot of people who didn't have health insurance on the job. So that meant that a lot of people just didn't bother getting health insurance at all. And when they got sick, they'd have to go to the emergency room.

AUDIENCE MEMBER: (Inaudible.)

THE PRESIDENT: Well, that's true, too.

And so you're relying on the emergency room, but the emergency room is the most expensive place to get care. And because you weren't insured, the hospital would have to give you the care for free, and they would have to then make up for those costs by charging everybody else more money. So it wasn't good for anybody.

So what the Affordable Care Act is designed to do is to help those people who were previously either uninsured or underinsured. And it worked to help those people in two ways.

First, we gave states funding to expand Medicaid to cover more people. In D.C. and the 31 states that took us up on that, more than 4 million people have coverage who didn't have it before. They now have health insurance.

Second, for people who made too much to qualify for Medicaid even after we expanded it, we set up what we call marketplaces on HealthCare.gov, so you could shop for a plan that fits your needs, and then we would give you tax credits to help you buy it. And most people today can find a plan for less than $75 a month at the HealthCare. gov marketplace when you include the tax credits that government is giving you. That means it's less than your cellphone bill -- because I know you guys are tweeting a lot -- (laughter) -- and texting and selfies. (Laughter.) And the good news is, is that most people who end up buying their coverage through the marketplaces, using these tax credits, are satisfied with their plans.

So not only did Obamacare do a lot of good for the 80-plus percent of Americans who already had health care, but now it gave a new affordable option to a lot of folks who never had options before. All told, about another 10 percent of the country now have coverage.

The Affordable Care Act has done what it was designed to do: It gave us affordable health care.

So what's the problem? Why is there still such a fuss? Well, part of the problem is the fact that a Democratic President named Barack Obama passed the law. (Applause.) And that's just the truth. (Laughter.) I mean, I worked really, really hard to engage Republicans; took Republican ideas that originally they had praised; said, let's work together to get this done. And when they just refused to do anything, we said, all right, we're going to have to do it with Democrats. And that's what we did.

And early on, Republicans just decided to oppose it. And then they tried to scare people with all kinds of predictions -- that it would be a job-killer; that it would force everyone into government-run insurance; that it would lead to rationing; that it would lead to death panels; that it would bankrupt the federal government. You remember all this. And despite the fact that all the bad things they predicted have not actually happened -- despite the fact that we've created more jobs since the bill passed in consecutive months than any time on record -- (applause) -- despite the fact that the uninsured rate has gone down to its lowest levels ever, despite that fact that it's actually cost less than anybody anticipated and has shown to be much less disruptive on existing plans that people get through their employers, despite the fact that it saved Medicare over $150 billion -- which makes that program more secure -- despite all this, it's been hard, if not impossible, for any Republican to admit it.

They just can't admit that a lot of good things have happened and the bad things they predicted didn't happen. So they just keep on repeating, we're going to repeal it. We're going to repeal it, and we're going to replace it with something better -- even though, six and a half years later, they haven't -- they still haven't shown us what it is that they would do that would be better.

But -- and this is actually the main reason I'm here -- just because a lot of the Republican criticism has proven to be false and politically motivated doesn't mean that there aren't some legitimate concerns about how the law is working now. And the main issue has to do with the folks who still aren't getting enough help. Remember, I said 80 percent of people, even before the law passed, already had health insurance. And then we expanded Medicaid, and we set up the marketplaces, and another 10 percent of people got health insurance. Well, but that still leaves that last 10 percent. And the fact that that last 10 percent still has difficulties is something that we've got to do something about.

Now, part of the reason for this is, as I already mentioned to you, not every state expanded Medicaid to its citizens, which means that some of the most vulnerable working families that the law was designed to help still haven't gotten insurance. As you may have heard, Florida is one of those states. If your governor could put politics aside --

AUDIENCE: Booo --

THE PRESIDENT: Don't boo -- vote. (Applause.)

If your governor would just put politics aside and do what's right, then more than 700,000 Floridians would suddenly have access to coverage. And, by the way, that would hold down costs for the rest of you, because there would be less uncompensated care in hospitals. And it means that people who did sign up for the marketplace, who oftentimes may be sicker, qualify for Medicaid and so they're not raising costs in the marketplace.

In fact, if the 19 states who so far have not expanded Medicaid would just do so, another 4 million people would have coverage right now all across the country.

So that's step number one. And that's, by the way, just completely in the control of these governors. They could be doing it -- right now. They could do it tomorrow.

Now, the second issue has to do with the marketplaces. Although the marketplaces are working well in most of the states, there are some states where there's still not enough competition between insurers. So if you only have one insurer, they may decide we're going to jack up rates because we can, because nobody else is offering a better price.

In those states where the governor or legislature is hostile to the ACA, it makes it harder to enroll people because the state is not actively participating in outreach. And so, as a consequence, in those states enrollment in the plan -- especially enrollment of young people -- has lagged.

And what that means is that the insurance pool is smaller and it gets a higher percentage of older and sicker people who are signing up -- because if you're sick or you're old, you're more likely to say, well, I'm going to sign up, no matter what, because I know I'm going to need it; if you're young and healthy like you guys, you say, eh, I'm fine, life is good -- so you have more older and sicker people signing up, fewer younger and healthier people signing up, and that drives rates up, because the people who use health care most end up being in the insurance pool; people who use it least are not.

And then, in some cases, insurers just set their prices too low at the outset because they didn't know what the insurance pool was going to look like, and then they started losing money. And so now they've decided to significantly increase premiums in some states.

Now, it's these premium increases in some of the states in the marketplace that sometimes attracts nega- tive headlines. Remember, these premium increases won't impact most of the people who are buying insurance through the marketplace, because even when premiums go up, the tax credits go up to offset the increases. So people who qualify for tax credits, they may not even notice their premiums went up because the tax credit is covered.

And keep in mind that these premium increases that some of you may have read about have no effect at all if you're getting health insurance on the job, or through

Medicaid or Medicare. So for the 80 [percent]-plus people who already had health insurance, if your premium is going up, it's not because of Obamacare. It's because of your employer or your insurer -- even though sometimes they try to blame Obamacare for why the rates go up. It's not because of any policy of the Affordable Care Act that the rates are going up.

But if you are one of the people who doesn't get health care on the job, doesn't qualify for Medicaid, doesn't qualify for Medicare -- doesn't qualify for a tax credit to help you buy insurance, because maybe you made just a little bit too much money under the law -- these premium increases do make insurance less affordable. And in some states, the premium increases are manageable. Some are 2 percent or 8 percent, some 20 percent. But we know there are some states that may see premiums go up by 50 percent or more.

And an extreme example is Arizona, where we expect benchmark premiums will more than double. Part of this is because Arizona is one of those states that had really low average premiums -- among the lowest in the country -- so now insurance companies basically are trying to catch up, and they also don't have a lot of competition there. And meanwhile, in states like Florida, the failure to expand Medicaid contributes to higher marketplace premiums. And then there are some other states that just because of the nature of their health care systems, or the fact that they're rural and people are dispersed, so it's harder to provide health care, more expensive -- they have a tougher time controlling costs generally.

Again, the tax credits in the ACA will protect most consumers from the brunt of these premium increases.

And with the ability to shop around on HealthCare.gov -- which works really well now -- most people can find plans for prices even lower than this year's prices. But there are going to be people who are hurt by premium increases or a lack of competition and choice. And I don't want to see anybody left out without health insurance. I don't want to see any family having to choose between health insurance now or saving for retirement, or saving for their kids' college education, or just paying their own bills.

So the question we should be asking is, what do we do about these growing pains in the Affordable Care Act, and how do we get the last 9 percent of Americans covered? How do we reach those last 9 percent? And how do we make sure that premiums are more stable going forward, and the marketplace insurance pools are more stable going forward?

Well, I can tell you what will not work. Repealing the Affordable Care Act will not work. (Applause.) That's a bad idea. That will not solve the problem. Because right off the bat, repeal would take away health care from 20 million people. We'd go back where 80 percent of people had health insurance instead of 90 percent -- right off the bat. And all the reforms that everybody benefits from that I talked about -- like young Americans being able to stay on their parents' plans, or the rules that prevent insurance companies from discriminating against people because of a preexisting condition like diabetes or cancer, or the rule now that you can't charge somebody more just because they're a woman -- all those reforms would go away for everybody, because that's part of Obamacare.

All the progress that we've made in controlling costs and improving how health care is delivered, progress that's helped hold growth in the price of health care to the slowest rate in 50 years -- all that goes away. That's what repeal means. It would be bad for everybody. And the majority of Americans, even if they don't know that they're benefitting from Obamacare, don't want to see these benefits and protections taken away from their families now that they have them. I guarantee you there are people who right now think they hate Obamacare. And if somebody told them, all right, we're repealing it, but now your kid who is on your plan is no longer on your plan, or now you've got a preexisting condition and you can't buy health insurance -- they'd be shocked. They'd be -- what do you mean?

So repeal is not the answer. Here is what we can do instead to actually make the Affordable Care Act work even better than it's working right now. And I've already mentioned one.

Florida and every state should expand Medicaid. (Applause.) Cover more people. It's easy to do, and it could be done right now. You'd cover 4 million more Americans, help drive down premiums for folks who buy insurance through the marketplace. And, by the way, because the federal government pays for almost all of this expansion, you can't use as an excuse that, well, the state can't afford it -- because the federal government is paying it. States like Louisiana that just expanded Medicaid -- you had a Republican governor replaced by a Democratic governor. He said, I want that money. Expanded Medicaid, and found not only does it insure more people, but it's actually saved the state big money and makes people less dependent on expensive emergency room care. So that's step number one.

Step number two. Since overall health care costs have turned out to be significantly lower than everyone expected since we passed Obamacare, since that's saved the federal government billions of dollars, we should use some of that money, some of those savings to now provide more tax credits for more middle-income families, for more young adults to help them buy insurance. It will make their premiums more affordable. And that's not just good for them -- it's good for everybody. Because when more people are in the marketplace, everybody will benefit from lower premiums. Healthier people, younger people start joining the pool; premiums generally go down. That would be number two.

The third thing we should do is add what's called a public plan fallback -- (applause) -- to give folks more options in those places where there are just not enough insurers to compete. And that's especially important in some rural communities and rural states and counties. If you live in L.A. right now, then it's working fine. There are a lot of insurers because it's a big market, there are a lot of providers. But if you're in some remote areas, or you're near some small towns, it may be that the economics of it just don't work unless the government is providing an option to make it affordable. And, by the way, this is not complicated. Basically, you would just wait and see -- if the private insurers are competing for business, then you don't have to trigger a public option. But if no private insurers are providing affordable insurance in an area, then the government would step in with a quality plan that people can afford.

And, by the way, this is not a radical idea. This idea is modeled on something that Republicans championed under George Bush for the Medicare Part D drug benefit program. It was fine when it was their idea. The fact that they're now opposed to it as some socialist scheme is not being consistent, it's being partisan.

And finally, we should continue to encourage innovation by the states. What the Affordable Care Act says is, here's how we propose you insure your populations, but you, the state, can figure out a different way to accomplish the same goal -- providing affordable, comprehensive coverage for the same number of residents at the same cost -- then go right ahead. There may be more than one way to skin a cat. Maybe you've got an idea we haven't thought of. Just show us, don't talk about it. Show us what the plan looks like.

Republicans who claim to care about your health insurance choices and your premiums, but then offer nothing and block common-sense solutions like the ones that I propose to improve them -- that's not right. And my message to them has been and will continue to be: Work with us. Make the system better. Help the people you serve. We're open to good ideas, but they've got to be real ideas -- not just slogans, not just votes to repeal. And they've got to pass basic muster. You can't say, well, if we just do -- if we just plant some magic beans -- (laughter) -- then everybody will have health insurance. No, we've got to have health care economists and experts look at it and see if the thing would actually work.

So that's where we are. Number one, Obamacare is helping millions of people right now. The uninsured rate has never been lower. It's helping everybody who already has health insurance, because it makes their policies better. Number two, there are still too many hardworking people who are not being reached by the law. Number three, if we tweak the program to reach those people who are not currently benefitting from the law, it will be good for them and it will be good for the country. Number four, if we repeal this law wholesale that will hurt the people who don't have coverage right now. It will hurt the 20 million who are already getting help through the law. And it will hurt the country as a whole.

So this should be an easy choice. All it does -- all it requires is putting aside ideology, and in good faith trying to implement the law of the land. And what we've learned, by the way, is that when governors and state legislators expand Medicaid for their citizens and they hold insurance companies accountable, and they're honest with unin- sured people about their options, and they're working with us on outreach, then the marketplace works the way it's supposed to. And when they don't, the marketplaces tend to have more problems. And that shouldn't be surprising. If state leaders purposely try to make something not work, then it's not going to run as smoothly as if they were trying to make it work. Common sense. You don't even have to go to Miami Dade to figure that out. (Laughter.)

The point is, now is not the time to move backwards on health care reform. Now is the time to move forward. The problems that may have arisen from the Affordable Care Act is not because government is too involved in the process. The problem is, is that we have not reached everybody and pulled them in. And think about it. When one of these companies comes out with a new smart- phone and it had a few bugs, what do they do? They fix it. They upgrade -- unless it catches fire, and they just -- (laughter) -- then they pull it off the market. But you don't go back to using a rotary phone. (Laughter.) You don't say, well, we're repealing smartphones -- we're just going to do the dial-up thing. (Laughter.) That's not what you do.

Well, the same basic principle applies here. We're not going to go back to discriminating against Americans with preexisting conditions. We're not going to go back to a time when people's coverage was dropped when they got sick. We're not going to go back to a situation where we're reinstating lifetime limits in the fine print so that you think you have insurance, and then you get really sick or you kid gets really sick, and you hit the limit that the insurance company set, and next thing you know they're not covering you anymore, and you got to figure out how you come up with another $100,000 or $200,000 to make sure that your child lives. We're not going to go back to that.

I hear Republicans in Congress object, and they'll say, no, no, no, no, we'll keep those parts of Obamacare that are popular; we'll just repeal everything else. Well, it turns out that the sum of those parts that are popular in Obamacare is Obamacare. (Applause.) It's just people don't always know it. And repealing it would make the majority of Americans worse off when it comes to health care.

And as I said, part of this is just -- you know, health care is complicated. Think about this speech -- it's been pretty long, and you're just -- you're thinking, wow, I just want to take a picture with the President or something. (Laughter.) So it's hard to get people focused on the facts. And even reporters who have covered this stuff -- and they do a good job; they're trying to follow all the debate. But a lot of times they just report, "Premium increases." And everybody thinks, wow, my insurance rates are going up, it must be Obama's fault -- even though you don't get health insurance through Obamacare, you get it through your job, and even though your increases have gone up a lot slower. Or suddenly you're paying a bigger copay, and, ah, thanks Obama. (Laughter.) Well, no, I had nothing to do with that.

So part of it is this is complicated, the way it gets reported. There's a lot of hysteria around anything that happens. And what we need to do is just focus on this very specific problem -- how do we make sure that more people are getting coverage, and folks right now who are not getting tax credits, aren't getting Medicaid, how do we help them, how do we reach them. And we can do it.

Instead of repealing the law, I believe the next President and the next Congress should take what we've learned over the past six years and in a serious way analyze it, figure out what it is that needs to get done, and make the Affordable Care Act better and cover even more people. But understand, no President can do it alone. We will need Republicans in Congress and in state governments to act responsibly and put politics aside. Because I want to remind you, a lot of the Affordable Care Act is built on Republican ideas.

In fact, Bernie Sanders is still mad at me because we didn't get single-payer passed. Now, we couldn't get single-payer passed, and I wanted to make sure that we helped as many people as possible, given the political constraints. And so we adopted a system that Republicans should like; it's based on a competitive, market-based system in which people have to a responsibility for themselves by buy insurance.

And maybe now that I'm leaving office, maybe Republicans can stop with the 60-something repeal votes they've taken, and stop pretending that they have a serious alternative, and stop pretending that all the terrible things they said would happen have actually happened, when they have not, and just work with the next President to smooth out the kinks.

Because it turns out, no major social innovation in America has ever worked perfectly at the start. Social Security didn't. Its benefits were stingy at first. It left out a whole lot of Americans. The same was true for Medicare. The same was true for Medicaid. The same was true for the prescription drug law. But what happened was, every year, people of goodwill from both parties tried to make it better. And that's what we need to do right now.

And I promise, if Republicans have good ideas to provide more coverage for folks like Amanda, I will be all for it. I don't care whose idea it is, I just want it to work. They can even change the name of the law to ReaganCare. (Laughter.) Or they can call it Paul Ryan Care. I don't care -- (laughter) -- about credit, I just want it to work because I care about the American people and making sure they've got health insurance.

But that brings me to my final point, and that is change does not typically come from the top down, it always comes from the bottom up. The Affordable Care Act was passed because the American people mobilized, not just to get me elected, but to keep the pressure on me to actually do something about health care and to put pressure on members of Congress to do something about it. And that's how change happens in America. It doesn't happen on its own. It doesn't happen from on high. It happens from the bottom up. And breaking gridlock will come only when the American people demand it.

So that's why I'm here. Only you can break this stalemate, but educating the public on the benefits of the Affordable Care Act, and then pressing your elected officials to do the right this and supporting elected officials who are doing the right things.

And this is one of the reasons why I'm so proud of what Miami-Dade College is doing, because it's making sure that students and faculty, and people throughout this community know about the law, know about how to sign up for health care, and then actually helps people sign up. And I'm incredibly proud of the leadership Joe Peña and the entire team in encouraging people to sign up.

Thanks to them, Miami-Dade has been hosting enrollment office hours and workshops, even on nights and weekends. Right here on the Wolfson campus, and on all the Miami-Dade campuses, you can go for a free one-on-one session where a trained expert can walk you through the process and answer any questions you have -- and then help you sign up for health care right there and then. Joe says he doesn't have a conversation without making sure people know how to get covered. The more young and healthy people like you who do the smart thing and sign up, then the better it's going to work for everybody.

And the good news is, in a few days, you can do just that because Open enrollment, the time when you can start signing up, begins on November 1. And you just need to go to HealthCare.gov, which works really well now. (Laughter.)

And campuses will be competing to come up with the most creative ways to reach people and get them signed up -- and I'm pretty sure that Miami-Dade can set the standard for the rest of the country. 'Cause that's how you do. (Applause.) That's how you do.

So much has changed since I campaigned here in Miami eight Octobers ago. But one thing has not: this is more than just about health care. It's about the character of our country. It's about whether we look out for one another. It's about whether the wealthiest nation on earth is going to make sure that nobody suffers. Nobody loses everything they have saved, everything they have worked for because they're sick. You stood up for the idea that no American should have to go without the health care they need.

And it's still true today. And we've proven together that people who love this country can change it -- 20 million people out there will testify. I get letters every day, just saying thank you because it's made a difference in their lives. And what true then is true now. We still need you. Our work to expand opportunity to all and make our union more perfect is never finished -- but the more we work, and organize, and advocate, and fight, the closer we get.

So I hope you are going to be busy this November signing folks up. But more importantly, I hope, for all the young people here, you never stop working for a better America. And even though I won't be President, I'll keep working right alongside you.

Thank you, everybody. God bless you. God bless America. Thank you. (Applause.)

1. According to President Obama, what issues in the health care system did the ACA seek to address?

"REMARKS BY PRESIDENT TRUMP ON HEALTHCARE," FROM THE WHITE HOUSE PRESS OFFICE, JUNE 13, 2017

THE PRESIDENT: Thank you. Thank you, everybody. Thank you very much.

Millions of American families — and I mean millions — continue to suffer from Obamacare while congressional Democrats obstruct our efforts to rescue them. And I'll tell you, that's exactly what's happening. The Democrats have let you down, big league. Standing beside me are two such families, representing so many others — millions of people — who have been victimized by Obamacare — terrible law.

My thanks to Michael and Tammy Kushman from Marinette County, and Robert and Sarah Stoll from Kenosha, as well as their wonderful families, for joining us today. We appreciate it. We appreciate all the people being here. Thank you, folks. (Applause.) They love their country, play by the rules, and work hard to give their loved ones the best life possible.

Michael Kushman is a proud veteran of the United States Army Medical Service Core. He and his wife Tammy were forced onto the Obamacare exchange in 2015 — and like countless others, they were shocked to learn that they couldn't keep their doctor as promised. They couldn't keep their plan as promised. They started out paying $600 per month. Then their insurer quit the exchange, so they had to switch to a new plan, and it went up to $1,000 a month. And it keeps going up and up and up. And that's where we are today. Now it's over $1,400 per month. They've been forced off their plans and onto a new one three times in three years. Their premiums have soared 127 percent. The Kushmans now spend nearly one-fourth of their net monthly income on health insurance. So — both of you, both families. Both great families.

Robert and his wife Sarah Stoll have also endured enormous pain under the crushing burden of Obamacare. Robert serves as a volunteer captain for the Randall Fire Department. He was a small business owner for 30 years. But their Obamacare premiums doubled, and Sarah was forced to leave retirement and find a part-time job just to pay the bills. When she did so, making matters worse, their new income meant they were no longer eligible for the tax credit they had once received — and the federal government actually forced them to repay thousands of dollars.

These are sad — I agree, that's true. Has it happened to you also? Yes. Yeah, it has. These are sad but familiar stories in Wisconsin, where Obamacare premiums have doubled. Obamacare is one of the greatest catastrophes that our country has signed into law — and the victims are innocent, hardworking Americans like Michael and Tammy, Robert and Sarah. These citizens deserve so much better.

The House of Representatives has passed on to the Senate, and the Senate is getting ready to do something — hopefully it will get done — where we will come up with a solution, and a really good one, to healthcare. No matter how good it is, we will get no obstructionist Democrat votes. No matter how good it is — if it's the greatest healthcare plan ever devised, we will get zero votes by the obstructionists, the Democrats. It's time to give American families quality, reliable, affordable healthcare — and that's what we are working very hard to do. And we'll get it done.

So I want to thank you, I want to thank the families — thank you very much — for being here. And I love being in Wisconsin. I love being in Wisconsin. Thank you. (Applause.)

1. According to President Trump, what were the problems with the ACA?

"REMARKS BY THE VICE PRESIDENT AND SECRETARY PRICE AT A ROUNDTABLE DISCUSSION ON HEALTHCARE," BY VICE PRESIDENT MIKE PENCE AND HEALTH SECRETARY TOM PRICE, FROM THE WHITE HOUSE PRESS OFFICE, JULY 21, 2017

VICE PRESIDENT PENCE: On behalf of the President, welcome to the White House.

I'm truly honored to be able to welcome organizations that literally represent millions of Americans and millions of businesses back here to the White House at such a critical time in our efforts to rescue the American people from the disastrous policies of Obamacare.

I'm grateful to be joined by groups ranging from the Chamber of Commerce and NFIB, to Concerned Women for America, the National Taxpayers Union, American Conservative Union, Club for Growth and the like. But thank you to each and every one of you for the way your organizations have stepped forward to make the case to the American people that we can repeal and replace Obamacare with policies that are built on freedom, that are built on state-based reform, and that will give the American people access to the world-class healthcare that they need and deserve.

As we gather today, we are just a few days away from a critical vote in the Congress, a vote to begin the debate on the repeal and replace of Obamacare. And President Trump and I are urging every member of the United States Senate to vote to begin this debate.

Every one of the groups that are gathered here today — the millions that you represent — are here to speak with one voice to say to the Congress: It's time to vote. It's time to act. It's time to get on with a debate to repeal and replace Obamacare.

As President Trump said when members of the Senate gathered here at the White House just a few short days ago, inaction is not an option. And frankly, as the President said, any senator who doesn't vote to begin the debate is essentially telling the American people that they're fine with Obamacare.

And that's just not acceptable because we all know the truth. Obamacare is collapsing all across the country as we speak. It's putting a burden on working families and American taxpayers and job creators all across this nation.

We all remember the broken promises of Obamacare. I have Dr. Price here. He and I were both members of Congress when the debate over Obamacare happened in the Congress seven years ago. I can still hear those promises ringing in my ears, can't you? If you like your doctor, you can keep them — not true. If you liked your health insurance, you can keep it — not true. The cost of health insurance would go down if Obamacare passed — not true.

We all know the facts. Even though we were promised that families would save $2,500 a year in premiums if Obamacare became law, according to our analysis at HHS, the average Obamacare plan today costs nearly $3,000 more than a plan did as recently as 2013. While premiums are soaring, choices are plummeting. Next year at least 40 percent of American counties, including nine entire states, will have only one choice of a health insurance provider, which is essentially no choice at all. And in many jurisdictions around the country, there's not even one choice. So the time has come for Congress to act.

The President and I are truly grateful to the organizations represented around here for lending your voices — voices for working families, voices for businesses large and small — to our effort to repeal and replace Obamacare. And we just urge you in the days that remain between now and this vote early next week to reach out to people across this country and let them know that we're close. We literally are just a few votes away from beginning a debate that will repeal and replace Obamacare in the United States Senate.

Congress needs to step up. Congress needs to do their job. And every member of the United States Senate should vote to begin the debate to rescue the American people from the disastrous policy of Obamacare, and we're grateful for your support.

With that, I want to recognize the Secretary of Health and Human Services, Dr. Tom Price, for this thoughts on this moment.

And let me just say this is a historic moment. For seven years, the American people have seen the broken promises of Obamacare, and we are just days away and a few short moments and just a few votes away from being able to keep a promise that every Republican in the Senate, every Republican in the House has made to the American people.

And our message today, our message to each one of you and the groups that you represent is make sure the American people know that it's time for Congress to act. And it's time for the American people to let their voice be heard. There is no voice more powerful in Washington, D.C. than the voice of the American people.

Tom?

SECRETARY PRICE: Thank you, Mr. Vice President. You're right, it is an historic moment. This is an historic room, and this an historic time for the American people and for your organizations.

I just want to thank you — lend my echoing words of the Vice President — but to thank each and every one of you for the productive and positive discussion and action that you have brought about over the past number of months. Time is of the essence. The fact is that the American people deserve and demand that Washington addresses their problems and their challenges, and this is a challenge that is not unknown to anybody who has been paying attention at all. And that is that the American people desire that healthcare be in the hands of people, in the hands of patients and their families and doctors — not in the hands of Washington, D.C. That's what this is all about.

There are decisions that will be made over the next few weeks in states all across this land about what 2018 looks like from an insurance standpoint, and the decision that is made in the next few days in this town will dictate and determine what those decisions will be. So as people are wont to say, this problem demands an act of Congress, and so it's an act of Congress that must happen. And we, once again, just can't thank you all enough for being that positive and productive influence on this discussion and this debate.

Thank you.

THE VICE PRESIDENT: Thank you, Tom. Let's send a very clear message in the days ahead that the beginning of the end of Obamacare is when Congress votes to start the debate on a bill that will repeal and replace this disastrous policy.

Early next week, every Republican in the Senate will be called upon to vote to begin the debate, and we urge each and every one of you on all the platforms that you have and all the millions of Americans that you reach to make sure every American knows that every Republican in the Senate should vote to begin the debate. Because once we begin the debate, the President and I are confident, working with all of you, working with the majority in the United States Senate that we will pass legislation out of the Senate, we will move this legislation forward, and we will rescue the American people from the disaster of Obamacare.

So let's go to work. Thank you all very much.

1. What problems did Republicans seek to address in the ACA, and with what solutions?

"WE FACT-CHECKED LAWMAKERS' LETTERS TO CONSTITUENTS ON HEALTH CARE," BY CHARLES ORNSTEIN, FROM *PROPUBLICA*, MARCH 22, 2017

THEY'RE FULL OF LIES AND MISINFORMATION

When Louisiana resident Andrea Mongler wrote to her senator, Bill Cassidy, in support of the Affordable Care Act, she wasn't surprised to get an email back detailing the law's faults. Cassidy, a Republican who is also a physician, has been a vocal critic.

"Obamacare" he wrote in January, "does not lower costs or improve quality, but rather it raises taxes and allows a presidentially handpicked 'Health Choices Commissioner' to determine what coverage and treatments are available to you."

There's one problem with Cassidy's ominous-sounding assertion: It's false.

The Affordable Care Act, commonly called Obamacare, includes no "Health Choices Commissioner." Another bill introduced in Congress in 2009 did include such a position, but the bill died — and besides, the job as outlined in that legislation didn't have the powers Cassidy ascribed to it.

As the debate to repeal the law heats up in Congress, constituents are flooding their representatives with notes of support or concern, and the lawmakers are responding, sometimes with form letters that are misleading. A review of more than 200 such letters by ProPublica and its partners at Kaiser Health News, Stat and Vox, found dozens of errors and mischaracterizations about the ACA and its proposed replacement. The legislators have cited wrong statistics, conflated health care terms and made statements that don't stand up to verification.

It's not clear if this is intentional or if the lawmakers and their staffs don't understand the current law or the proposals to alter it. Either way, the issue of what is wrong — and right — about the current system has become critical as the House prepares to vote on the GOP's replacement bill Thursday.

"If you get something like that in writing from your U.S. senator, you should be able to just believe that," said Mongler, 34, a freelance writer and editor who is pursuing a master's degree in public health. "I hate that people are being fed falsehoods, and a lot of people are buying it and not questioning it. It's far beyond politics as usual."

Cassidy's staff did not respond to questions about his letter.

Political debates about complex policy issues are prone to hyperbole and health care is no exception. And to be sure, many of the assertions in the lawmakers' letters are at least partially based in fact.

Democrats, for instance, have been emphasizing to their constituents that millions of previously uninsured people now have medical coverage thanks to the law. They say insurance companies can no longer discriminate against millions of patients with pre-existing conditions. And they credit the law with allowing adults under age 26 to stay on their parents' health plans. All true.

For their part, Republicans criticize the law for not living up to its promises. They say former President Obama pledged that people could keep their health plans and doctors and premiums would go down. Neither has happened. They also say that insurers are dropping out of the market and that monthly premiums and deductibles (the amount people must pay before their coverage kicks in) have gone up. All true.

But elected officials in both parties have incorrectly cited statistics and left out important context. We decided to take a closer look after finding misleading statements in an email Sen. Roy Blunt, R-Mo., sent to his constituents. We solicited letters from the public and found a wealth of misinformation, from statements that were simply misleading to whoppers. More Republicans fudged than Democrats, though both had their moments.

An aide to Rep. Dana Rohrabacher, R-Calif., defended his hyperbole as "within the range of respected interpretations."

"Do most people pay that much attention to what their congressman says? Probably not," said Sherry Glied, dean of New York University's Robert F. Wagner Graduate School of Public Service, who served as an assistant Health and Human Services secretary from 2010 to 2012. "But I think misinformation or inaccurate information is a bad thing and not knowing what you're voting on is a really bad thing."

We reviewed the emails and letters sent by 51 senators and 134 members of the House within the past few months. Here are some of the most glaring errors and omissions:

REP. PAT TIBERI, R-OHIO, INCORRECTLY CITED THE NUMBER OF OHIO COUNTIES THAT HAD ONLY ONE INSURER ON THE AFFORDABLE CARE ACT INSURANCE EXCHANGE.

What he wrote: "In Ohio, almost one third of counties will have only one insurer participating in the exchange."

What's misleading: In fact, only 23 percent (less than one quarter) had only one option, according to an analysis by the Kaiser Family Foundation.

His response: A Tiberi spokesperson defended the statement. "The letter says 'almost' because only 9 more counties in Ohio need to start offering only 1 plan on the exchanges to be one third."

Why his response is misleading: Ohio has 88 counties. A 10 percent difference is not "almost."

REP. KEVIN YODER, R-KAN., SAID THAT THE QUALITY OF HEALTH CARE IN THE COUNTRY HAS DECLINED BECAUSE OF THE ACA, OFFERING NO PROOF.

What he wrote: "Quality of care has decreased as doctors have been burdened with increased regulations on their profession."

Why it's misleading: Some data shows that health care has improved after the passage of the ACA. Patients are less likely to be readmitted to a hospital within 30 days after they have been discharged, for instance. Also, payments have been increasingly linked to patients' outcomes rather than just the quantity of services delivered. A 2016 report by the Commonwealth Fund, a health care nonprofit think tank, found that the quality care has improved in many communities following the ACA.

His response: None.

REP. ANNA ESHOO, D-CALIF., MISSTATED THE PERCENTAGE OF MEDICAID SPENDING THAT COVERS THE COST OF LONG-TERM CARE, SUCH AS NURSING HOME STAYS.

What she wrote: "It's important to note that 60 percent of Medicaid goes to long-term care and with the evisceration of it in the bill, this critical coverage is severely compromised."

What's misleading: Medicaid does not spend 60 percent of its budget on long-term care. The figure is closer to a quarter, according to the Center on Budget and Policy Priorities, a liberal think tank. Medicaid does, however, cover more than 60 percent of all nursing home residents.

Her response: Eshoo's office said the statistic was based on a subset of enrollees who are dually enrolled in Medicaid and Medicare. For this smaller group, 62 percent of Medicaid expenditures were for long-term support services, according to the Kaiser Family Foundation.

What's misleading about the response: Eshoo's letter makes no reference to this population, but instead refers to the 75 million Americans on Medicaid.

REP. CHUCK FLEISCHMANN, R-TENN., POINTED TO THE NUMBER OF UNINSURED AMERICANS AS A FAILURE OF THE ACA, WITHOUT NOTING THAT THE LAW HAD DRAMATICALLY REDUCED THE NUMBER OF UNINSURED.

What he wrote: "According to the U.S. Census Bureau, approximately thirty-three million Americans are still living without health care coverage and many more have coverage that does not adequately meet their health care needs."

Why it's misleading: The actual number of uninsured in 2015 was about 29 million, a drop of 4 million from the prior year, the Census Bureau reported in September. Fleischmann's number was from the previous year.

Beyond that, reducing the number of uninsured by more than 12 million people from 2013 to 2015 has been seen as a success of Obamacare. And the Republican repeal-and-replace bill is projected to increase the number of uninsured.

His response: None.

REP. JOSEPH P. KENNEDY III, D-MASS., OVERSTATED THE NUMBER OF YOUNG ADULTS WHO WERE ABLE TO STAY ON THEIR PARENTS' HEALTH PLAN AS A RESULT OF THE LAW.

What he wrote: The ACA "allowed 6.1 million young adults to remain covered by their parents' insurance plans."

What's misleading: A 2016 report by the U.S. Department

of Health and Human Services, released during the Obama administration, however, pegged the number at 2.3 million.

Kennedy may have gotten to 6.1 million by including 3.8 million young adults who gained health insurance coverage through insurance marketplaces from October 2013 through early 2016.

His response: A spokeswoman for Kennedy said the office had indeed added those two numbers together and would fix future letters.

REP. BLAINE LUETKEMEYER, R-MO., SAID THAT 75 PERCENT OF HEALTH INSURANCE MARKETPLACES RUN BY STATES HAVE FAILED. THEY HAVE NOT.

What he said: "Nearly 75 percent of state-run exchanges have already collapsed, forcing more than 800,000 Americans to find new coverage."

What's misleading: When the ACA first launched, 16 states and the District of Columbia opted to set up their own exchanges for residents to purchase insurance, instead of using the federal marketplace, known as Healthcare.gov.

Of the 16, four state exchanges, in Oregon, Hawaii, New Mexico and Nevada, failed, and Kentucky plans to close its exchange this year, according to a report by the House Energy and Commerce Committee. While the report casts doubt on the viability of other state exchanges, it is clear that three-quarters have not failed.

His response: None.

REP. DANA ROHRABACHER, R-CALIF., OVERSTATED THAT THE ACA "DISTORTED LABOR MARKETS," PROMPTING EMPLOYERS TO SHIFT WORKERS FROM FULL-TIME JOBS TO PART-TIME JOBS.

What he said: "It has also, through the requirement that employees that work thirty hours or more be considered full time and thus be offered health insurance by their employer, distorted the labor market."

What's misleading: A number of studies have found little to back up that assertion. A 2016 study published by the journal Health Affairs examined data on hours worked, reason for working part time, age, education and health insurance status. "We found only limited evidence to support this speculation" that the law led to an increase in part-time employment, the authors wrote. Another study found much the same.

In addition, PolitiFact labeled as false a statement last June by President Donald Trump in which he said, "Because of Obamacare, you have so many part-time jobs."

His response: Rohrabacher spokesman Ken Grubbs said the congressman's statement was based on an article that said, "Are Republicans right that employers are capping workers' hours to avoid offering health insurance? The evidence suggests the answer is 'yes,' although the number of workers affected is fairly small."

We pointed out that "fairly small" was hardly akin to distorting the labor market. To which Grubbs replied, "The congressman's letter is well within the range of respected interpretations. That employers would react to Obamacare's impact in such way is so obvious, so nearly axiomatic, that it is pointless to get lost in the weeds," Grubbs said.

REP. MIKE BISHOP, R-MICH., APPEARS TO HAVE CITED A SPECULATIVE 2013 REPORT BY A GOP-LED HOUSE COMMITTEE AS EVIDENCE OF CURRENT AND FUTURE PREMIUM INCREASES UNDER THE ACA.

What he wrote: "Health insurance premiums are slated to increase significantly. Existing customers can expect an average increase of 73 percent, while the average change due to Obamacare for those purchasing a new plan will be a 96 percent increase in premiums. The average cost for a new customer in the individual market is expected to rise $1,812 per year."

What's misleading: The figures seem to have come from a report issued before the Obamacare insurance marketplaces launched and before 2014 premiums had been announced. The letter implies these figures are current. In fact, premium increases by and large have been moderate under Obamacare. The average monthly premium for a benchmark plan, upon which federal subsidies are calculated, increased about 2 percent from 2014 to 2015; 7 percent from 2015 to 2016; and 25 percent this year, for states that take part in the federal insurance marketplace.

His response: None

REP. DAN NEWHOUSE, R-WASH., MISSTATED THE REASONS WHY MEDICAID COSTS PER PERSON WERE HIGHER THAN EXPECTED IN 2015.

What he wrote: "A Medicaid actuarial report from August 2016 found that the average cost per enrollee was 49 percent higher than estimated just a year prior — in large part due to beneficiaries seeking care at more expensive hospital emergency rooms due to difficulty finding a doctor and long waits for appointments."

What's misleading: The report did not blame the higher costs on the difficulty patients had finding doctors. Among the reasons the report did cite: patients who were sicker than anticipated and required a raft of services after being previously uninsured. The report also noted that costs are expected to decrease in the future.

His response: None

SEN. DICK DURBIN, D-ILL., WRONGLY STATED THAT FAMILY PREMIUMS ARE DECLINING UNDER OBAMACARE.

What he wrote: "Families are seeing lower premiums on their insurance, seniors are saving money on prescription drug costs, and hospital readmission rates are dropping."

What's misleading: Durbin's second and third points are true. The first, however, is misleading. Family insurance premiums have increased in recent years, although with government subsidies, some low- and middle-income families may be paying less for their health coverage than they once did.

His response: Durbin's office said it based its statement on an analysis published in the journal Health Affairs that said that individual health insurance premiums dropped between 2013 and 2014, the year that Obamacare insurance marketplaces began. It also pointed to a *Washington Post* opinion piece that said that premiums under the law are lower than they would have been without the law.

Why his response is misleading: The *Post* piece his office cites states clearly, "Yes, insurance premiums are going up, both in the health care exchanges and in the employer-based insurance market."

REP. SUSAN BROOKS, R-IND., TOLD CONSTITUENTS THAT PREMIUMS NATIONWIDE WERE SLATED TO JUMP FROM 2016 TO 2017, BUT FAILED TO MENTION THAT PREMIUMS FOR SOME PLANS IN HER HOME STATE ACTUALLY DECREASED.

What she wrote: "Since the enactment of the ACA, deductibles are up, on average, 63 percent. To make matters worse, monthly premiums for the "bronze plan" rose 21 percent from 2016 to 2017. … Families and individuals covered through their employer are forced to make the difficult choice: pay their premium each month or pay their bills."

What's misleading: Brooks accurately cited national data from the website HealthPocket, but her statement is misleading. Indiana was one of two states in which the premium for a benchmark health plan — the plan used to calculate federal subsidies — actually went down between 2016 and 2017. Moreover, more than 80 percent of marketplace consumers in Indiana receive subsidies *that lowered* their premium costs. The HealthPocket figures refer to people who do not qualify for those subsidies.

Her response: Brooks' office referred to a press release from Indiana's Department of Insurance, which took issue with an Indianapolis Star story about premiums going down. The release, from October, when Vice President Mike Pence was Indiana's governor, said that the average premiums would go up more than 18 percent over 2016 rates based on enrollment at that time. In addition, the release noted, 68,000 Indiana residents lost their health plans when their insurers withdrew from the market.

Why her response is misleading: For Indiana consumers who shopped around, which many did, there was an opportunity to find a cheaper plan.

SEN. RON WYDEN, D-ORE., INCORRECTLY SAID THAT THE REPUBLICAN BILL TO REPEAL OBAMACARE WOULD CUT FUNDING FOR SENIORS IN NURSING HOMES.

What he wrote: "It's terrible for seniors. Trumpcare forces older Americans to pay 5 times the amount younger Americans will — an age tax — and slashes Medicaid benefits for nursing home care that two out of three Americans in nursing homes rely on."

What's misleading: Wyden is correct that the GOP bill, known as the American Health Care Act, would allow insurance companies to charge older adults five times higher premiums than younger ones, compared to three times higher premiums under the existing law. However, it does not directly slash Medicaid benefits for nursing home residents. It proposes cutting Medicaid funding and giving states a greater say in setting their own priorities. States may, as a result, end up cutting services, jeopardizing nursing home care for poor seniors, advocates say, because it is one of the most expensive parts of the program.

His response: Taylor Harvey, a spokesman for Wyden, defended the statement, noting that the GOP health bill cuts Medicaid funding by $880 billion over 10 years and places a cap on spending. "Cuts to Medicaid would force states to nickel and dime nursing homes, restricting access to care for older Americans and making it a benefit in name only," he wrote.

Why his response is misleading: The GOP bill does not spell out how states make such cuts.

REP. DEREK KILMER, D-WASH., MISLEADINGLY SAID PREMIUMS WOULD RISE UNDER THE OBAMACARE REPLACEMENT BILL NOW BEING CONSIDERED BY THE HOUSE.

What he wrote: "It's about the 24 million Americans expected to lose their insurance under the Trumpcare plan and for every person who will see their insurance premiums rise — on average 10-15 percent."

Why it's misleading: First, the Congressional Budget Office did estimate that the GOP legislation would cover 24 million fewer Americans by 2026. But not all of those people would "lose their insurance." Some would choose to drop coverage because the bill would no longer make it mandatory to have health insurance, as is the case now.

Second, the budget office did say that in 2018 and 2019, premiums under the GOP bill would be 15-20 percent higher than they would have been under Obamacare because the share of unhealthy patients would increase as some of those who are healthy drop out. But it noted that after that, premiums would be lower than under the ACA.

His response: "It is indisputable that the nonpartisan Congressional Budget Office has said 24 million fewer people will have health care under the D.C. Republican plan. Whether folks lose their insurance or choose not to buy it because of sticker shock, having fewer people in the health care system is a bad outcome for all Americans," said Kilmer spokesman Jason Phelps in an email. "It is also a fact that the CBO has estimated premiums will go up by as much as 15% in the short term. President Trump pledged that his health care plan would provide 'insurance for everybody' and be 'much less expensive.'"

1. Based on this article, what are some of the common issues on which politicians make misleading points regarding the ACA?

2. How does this kind of misleading information influence the way we talk about and understand health care access?

WHAT THE COURTS SAY

In recent years, the courts have weighed in on health care issues with considerable impact on how we think about these questions moving forward. The Supreme Court is a crucial source for precedent when it comes to legislation, and the limitations their decisions place on health care laws create precedent that will impact future legislation for generations to come. But the courts hear cases that ask questions more complex than simply whether we should have access to health care. Issues like religious freedom or how taxes are levied intersect with the health care debate, as well as individual rights and corporate responsibility. The court cases below remind us of the relationship between these varied subjects, and show the complex way our political culture influences health care.

EXCERPT FROM "PETITION FOR A WRIT OF CERTIORARI TO THE UNITED STATES COURT OF APPEALS FOR THE ELEVENTH CIRCUIT: *UNITED STATES DEPARTMENT OF HEALTH AND HUMAN SERVICES, ET AL., PETITIONERS V STATE OF FLORIDA, ET AL.*," FROM THE US SUPREME COURT, AUGUST 12, 2011

STATEMENT

1. Congress enacted the Patient Protection and Affordable Care Act, Pub. L. No. 111-148, 124 Stat. 119 (Affordable Care Act or Act)[1], to address a profound and enduring crisis in the market for health care that accounts for more than 17% of the Nation's gross domestic product. Millions of people do not have health insurance yet actively participate in the health care market. They consume health care services for which they do not pay, and thus shift billions of dollars of health care costs to other market participants. The result is higher insurance premiums that, in turn, make insurance unaffordable to even greater numbers of people. At the same time, insurance companies use restrictive underwriting practices to deny coverage or charge more to millions of people because of pre-existing medical conditions.

    a. In the Affordable Care Act, Congress addressed these problems through a comprehensive program of economic regulation and tax measures. The Act includes provisions designed to make affordable health insurance more widely available, to protect consumers from restrictive insurance underwriting practices, and to reduce the uncompensated costs of medical care obtained by the uninsured.

First, the Act builds upon the existing nationwide system of employer-based health insurance that is the principal private mechanism for financing health care. The Act establishes new tax incentives for small businesses to purchase health insurance for their employees, 26 U.S.C.A 45R^2, and, under certain circumstances, prescribes tax penalties for large employers that do not offer adequate coverage to full-time employees, 26 U.S.C.A. 4980H (employer responsibility provision).

Second, the Act provides for the creation of health insurance exchanges to allow individuals, families, and small businesses to leverage their collective buying power to obtain health insurance at rates that are competitive with those of typical employer group plans.

Third, the Act establishes federal tax credits to assist eligible households with incomes from 133% to 400% of the federal poverty level to purchase insurance through the exchanges. 26 U.S.C.A. 36B. In addition, the Act expands eligibility for Medicaid to cover individuals with income below 133% of the federal poverty level. 42 U.S.C.A. 1396a(a)(10)(A)(i)(VIII). The Act provides that the federal government will pay 100% of the expenditures required to cover these newly eligible Medicaid recipients through 2016. 42 U.S.C.A.1396d(y)(1). The federal government's share will then decline slightly and level off at 90% in 2020 and beyond—far above the usual federal matching rates under Medicaid. *Ibid.*

Fourth, the Act regulates insurers to prohibit industry practices that have prevented individuals from obtaining and maintaining health insurance. The Act will bar insurers from refusing coverage because of a pre-existing medical condition, 42 U.S.C.A. 300gg-1(a), 300gg-3(a) (the guaranteed-issue provision), thereby guaranteeing insurance to many previously unable to obtain it. The Act also bars insurers from charging higher premiums based on a person's medical history, 42 U.S.C.A. 300gg (the community-rating provision), requiring instead that premiums generally be based on community-wide criteria.

Fifth, the Act amends the Internal Revenue Code to provide that a non-exempted individual who fails to maintain a minimum level of health insurance must pay a tax penalty. 26 U.S.C.A. 5000A (the minimum coverage provision). That insurance requirement, which takes effect in 2014, 26 U.S.C.A. 5000A(a), may be satisfied through enrollment in an employer-sponsored insurance plan; an individual plan, including one offered through a new health insurance exchange; a grandfathered health plan; a government-sponsored program such as Medicare or Medicaid; or similar federally recognized coverage, 26 U.S.C.A. 5000A(f).

The amount of the tax penalty owed under the minimum coverage provision is calculated as a percentage of household income, subject to a floor and capped at the price of forgone insurance coverage. The penalty is reported on the individual's federal income tax return and is assessed and collected in the same manner as certain other assessable tax penalties under the Internal Revenue Code. Individuals who are not required to file income tax returns for a given year are not required to pay the tax penalty. 26 U.S.C.A. 5000A(b)(2), (c)(1) and (2), (e)(2) and (g).

The Congressional Budget Office (CBO) has projected that, by 2017, the Affordable Care Act will reduce the number of non-elderly individuals without insurance by about 33 million. *CBO's March 2011 Estimate of the Effects of the Insurance Coverage Provisions Contained in the Patient Protection and Affordable Care Act 1* (Mar. 18, 2011). The CBO has attributed approximately half of the projected decrease in the number of nonelderly uninsured—16 million people—to the minimum coverage provision. CBO, *Effects of Eliminating the Individual Mandate to Obtain Health Insurance 2* (June 16, 2010) (*Eliminating Individual Mandate*).

b. Congress expressly found that the minimum coverage provision "regulates activity that is commercial and economic in nature," namely "how and when health care is paid for, and when health insurance is purchased." 42 U.S.C.A. 18091(a)(2)(A). That assessment reflects a number of realities about the health care market.

First, participation in the market for health care is virtually universal. Nearly everyone obtains health care services at some point, and most do so each year. Moreover, every individual is always at risk of requiring health care, and the need for particularly expensive services is unpredictable. "Most medical expenses for people under 65" result "from the 'bolt-from-the-blue' event of an accident, a stroke, or a complication of pregnancy that we know will happen on average but whose victim we cannot (and they cannot) predict well in advance." *Expanding Consumer Choice and Addressing "Adverse Selection" Concerns in Health Insurance: Hearing Before the Joint Economic Comm.*, 108th Cong., 2d Sess. 32 (2004) (Prof. Mark V. Pauly). Costs can mount rapidly for even the most common medical procedures, making it difficult for all, and impossible for many, to budget for such contingencies.

Because the timing and magnitude of health care expenses are so difficult to predict and thus give rise to an ever-present risk, health insurance is the customary means of financing health care purchases and protecting against the attendant risks. In 2009, payments by private and government insurers constituted 71% of national health care spending. Centers for Medicare & Medicaid Servs., *2009 National Health Expenditure Data*, Tbl. 3 (2011).

Yet millions of Americans do not have health insurance, either public or private, and instead attempt to self-insure. They actively participate in the health care market regardless of their ability to pay. When people "forego health insurance coverage and attempt to selfinsure," they typically fail to pay the full cost of the services they consume, and they shift the costs of their uncompen-sated care—totaling $43 billion in 2008—to health care providers. 42 U.S.C.A. 18091(a)(2)(A) and (F). Congress found that providers in turn pass on a significant portion of those costs "to private insurers, which pass on the cost to families," increasing the average premium for insured families by "over $1,000 a year." 42 U.S.C.A. 18091(a)(2)(F).

This cost-shifting occurs in large part because, unlike in other markets, those who cannot afford to pay for emergency health care from commercial providers receive it anyway. Numerous state legislatures and courts, including those in a number of respondent States, have concluded that hospitals cannot properly turn away people in need of emergency treatment. See H.R. Rep. No. 241, 99th Cong., 1st Sess. Pt. 3, at 5 (1985); App. 248a (Marcus, J., dissenting).

Reflecting the same moral judgment, the federal Emergency Medical Treatment and Labor Act requires hospitals that participate in the Medicare program and offer emergency services to stabilize any patient who arrives with an emergency condition, regardless of whether the person has insurance or otherwise can pay. 42 U.S.C. 1395dd.

In addition to finding that the minimum coverage provision regulates economic activity having a substantial effect on interstate commerce, 42 U.S.C.A. 18091(a) (2)(A), Congress found that the provision is necessary to achieving the goals of the Act's guaranteed issue and community-rating insurance reforms. Those provisions will require that insurers provide coverage and charge premiums without regard to a person's medical history. Evidence from economists, insurers, and state regulators established that, absent an ongoing requirement to maintain a minimum amount of coverage, that new ability to obtain insurance regardless of medical history, and at rates independent of health status, would enable "many individuals [to] wait to purchase health insurance until they needed care." 42 U.S.C.A. 18091(a)(2)(I). That dynamic would undermine the effective functioning of insurance markets. Accordingly, Congress found the minimum coverage requirement "essential to creating effective health insurance markets in which improved health insurance products that are guaranteed issue and do not exclude coverage of preexisting conditions can be sold." *Ibid.*

2. Respondents are two individuals, Mary Brown and Kaj Ahlburg; the National Federation of Independent Business (NFIB), of which Brown is a member; and 26

States. They filed suit in the Northern District of Florida, challenging the constitutionality of several provisions of the Affordable Care Act.

The district court determined that at least one individual respondent, Brown, has standing to challenge the minimum coverage provision because she does not currently have health insurance and must "make financial arrangements now to ensure compliance" with the minimum coverage provision in 2014. App. 292a. The court also held that two respondent States, Idaho and Utah, have standing to challenge the minimum coverage provision because they enacted statutes purporting to exempt their residents from it. App. 293a-295a. The district court also concluded that the Anti-Injunction Act, 26 U.S.C. 7421(a), does not bar this suit. App. 401a425a.

Addressing the merits, the district court held that the minimum coverage provision is not a valid exercise of Congress's commerce or taxing powers. App. 278a n.4, 296a-350a, 401a-424a. The court rejected, however, the individual respondents' contention that the minimum coverage provision also violates substantive due process, App. 465a-468a, as well as the state respondents' challenges to the Medicaid eligibility expansion, App. 280a288a, the provisions for establishing health insurance exchanges, App. 452a-455a, and, as applied to them as employers, the employer responsibility provision, App. 445a-451a. The court nonetheless held the entire Act invalid because it concluded that the minimum coverage provision could not be severed from any other provision in the statute. App. 350a-364a. The court stayed its declaratory judgment pending appellate review. App. 387a-392a.

3. a. A divided court of appeals affirmed in part and reversed in part. As a threshold matter, the court held that respondent Brown has standing to challenge the minimum coverage provision, but declined to decide whether the respondent States also have standing to challenge it, calling that a "difficult" question. App. 9a. On the merits, the court rejected the respondent States' challenge to the constitutionality of the expansion of Medicaid eligibility, App. 50a-63a, but held that the minimum coverage provision is not a valid exercise of Congress's commerce power, App. 63a-156a, or taxing power, App. 157a-172a. The court reversed the district court's conclusion that the entire Act is inseverable from the minimum coverage provision and held that the remainder of the Act could stand. App. 172a-186a.

The majority recognized that individuals without insurance participate in the health care market, and that, as a class, they annually consume billions of dollars of health care services for which they do not pay. App. 11a. The majority also recognized that the consumption of such uncompensated health care imposes a substantial burden on interstate commerce: health care providers shift the costs of uncompensated care to insurers, which in turn shift those costs to other consumers in the form of higher premiums. App. 11a-12a.

The majority further acknowledged (as respondents had conceded) that the Commerce Clause would plainly permit Congress to regulate the way people pay for health care services at the time that they obtain such services. App. 118a. The majority took issue only with the timing of the insurance requirement in the minimum coverage provision, declaring that provision invalid because it "does *not* regulate behavior at the point of consumption." *Ibid.* The majority declared that the minimum coverage provision is "overinclusive in *when* it regulates: it conflates those who presently consume health care with those who will not consume health care for many years into the future." App. 119a.

In addition, the majority opined, Congress could have achieved its regulatory objectives without the minimum coverage provision. App. 127a-128a. In the majority's view, other provisions of the Act, such as the guaranteed-issue and community-rating requirements, will significantly reduce the number of uninsured persons and the costs they shift to other market participants. App. 127a-128a. The majority acknowledged Congress's finding that the minimum coverage provision is "essential" to the success of those other provisions. App. 148a (quoting 42 U.S.C.A. 18091a(2)(I)). And it also did not dispute the experience of state regulators, which demonstrated that, in the absence of a minimum coverage requirement, individuals would often "delay purchasing private insurance until an acute medical need arises," thereby rendering their guaranteed-issue and community-rating reforms ineffective. App. 148a; see App. 230a-231a (Marcus, J., dissenting). The court nonetheless declined to uphold the minimum coverage provision as part of a "broader regulation of the insurance market." App. 148a.

The court of appeals also held that the minimum coverage provision is not a proper exercise of Congress's Article I taxing power. The court acknowledged that the provision amends the Internal Revenue Code to provide that non-exempted individuals who fail to maintain minimum coverage shall pay a penalty that is calculated as a percentage of their household incomes (above a flat dollar amount and below a cap), reported on their individual federal income tax returns, and assessed and collected by the Internal Revenue Service. App. 38a, 44a45a. And the court did not question projections that the minimum coverage provision will generate billions in revenue each year. App. 168a. The court nonetheless held that Congress's taxing power did not provide a constitutional basis for the provision because the Act uses the term "penalty," not "tax," to describe the assessment. App. 169a.

The court declared the minimum coverage provision severable from the rest of the Act. App. 186a. It concluded that the guaranteed-issue and community-rating provisions were capable of functioning independently and (together with the other provisions of the Act) would sufficiently advance the Act's "basic objective * * * to make health insurance coverage accessible and thereby to reduce the number of uninsured persons." App. 180a186a.

b. Judge Marcus dissented from the majority's Commerce Clause ruling. His analysis relied in part on the Sixth Circuit's decision in *Thomas More Law Ctr. v. Obama*, No. 10-2388, 2011 WL 2556039 (June 29, 2011), petition for cert. pending, No. 11-117 (filed July 26, 2011), and, in particular, on Judge Sutton's concurring opinion in that case. Judge Marcus reasoned that the minimum coverage provision regulates "quintessentially economic conduct"—the timing and method by which individuals pay for health care. App. 189a, 194a-195a. He observed that "substantial numbers of uninsured Americans are currently active participants in the health care services market, and that many of these uninsured currently consume health care services for which they cannot or do not pay." App. 213a. He explained that "[t]his is, in every real and meaningful sense, classic economic *activity*, which, as Congress' findings tell us, has a profound effect on commerce." *Ibid.*

Judge Marcus further explained that the minimum coverage provision is essential to the Act's guaranteed issue and community-rating reforms because, without a requirement to obtain insurance, those new protections would allow people to delay the purchase of insurance until they develop acute medical needs. App. 196a, 230a231a. Judge Marcus therefore reasoned that "Congress had more than 'a rational basis for concluding'" that the requirement was "essential to the success of the Act's concededly valid and quintessentially economic insurer reforms." App. 241a (quoting *Gonzales v. Raich*, 545 U.S. 1, 19 (2005)).

REASONS FOR GRANTING THE PETITION

The court of appeals has held unconstitutional a central provision of the Affordable Care Act, which represents the considered judgment of the elected Branches of Government—after years of study and deliberation—on how to address a crisis in the national health care market. That crisis has put the cost of health insurance beyond the reach of millions of Americans, and has denied coverage entirely to millions more. The Act is a comprehensive statute that builds on the system of private and public insurance to finance health care. It utilizes various regulatory and tax measures to reform insurance practices, extend coverage, and address other problems in the health care market.

The Act requires that non-exempted individuals finance their health care consumption through insurance, rather than rely on a combination of attempted self insurance and the back-stop of care paid for by other market participants. The minimum coverage provision, like the Act as a whole, thus regulates economic conduct that substantially affects interstate commerce. The provision is also integral to the rules Congress prescribed to end discriminatory insurance practices that deny coverage to, or increase rates for, millions of Americans with preexisting medical conditions. Further, the minimum coverage provision is effectuated by means of a penalty that operates as a tax, payable only by those who are required to file income tax returns and based on their adjusted gross income. For these reasons, the minimum coverage provision is squarely within Congress's power to regulate interstate commerce, lay and collect taxes, and enact legislation that is necessary and proper to effectuate its enumerated powers.

The court of appeals' contrary decision is fundamentally flawed and denies Congress the broad deference it is due in enacting laws to address the Nation's most pressing economic problems and set tax policy. The importance of the decision below—which strikes down "a central piece of a comprehensive economic regulatory scheme enacted by Congress," App. 189a (Marcus, J., dissenting), on a ground that has no basis in the Constitution's text or this Court's precedents—is manifest. Moreover, the court of appeals' conclusion that the minimum coverage provision lies outside Congress's commerce authority directly conflicts with a recent decision of the Sixth Circuit. See *Thomas More Law Ctr. v. Obama*, No. 10-2388, 2011 WL 2556039, at *8-*15 (June 29, 2011) (opinion of Martin, J.), *21-*33 (Sutton, J., concurring in the judgment) (*Thomas More*), petition for cert. pending, No. 11-117 (filed July 26, 2011). Review by this Court is plainly warranted.

A. THE COURT OF APPEALS' CONCLUSION THAT THE MINIMUM COVERAGE PROVISION IS BEYOND CONGRESS'S ARTICLE I POWER WARRANTS THIS COURT'S REVIEW

1. THE DECISION BELOW MISCONSTRUES CONGRESS'S COMMERCE CLAUSE AUTHORITY AND DISREGARDS THE NATURE OF THE HEALTH CARE MARKET

The Constitution confers on Congress the power to "regulate Commerce * * * among the several States." Art. I, § 8, Cl. 3. That power includes the authority to regulate intrastate conduct that has "a substantial effect on interstate commerce." *Gonzales v. Raich*, 545 U.S. 1, 17 (2005). In reviewing the validity of Commerce Clause legislation, a court's task "is a modest one." *Id.* at 22. The court "need not determine" whether the regulated conduct, "taken in the aggregate, substantially affect[s] interstate commerce in fact, but only whether a 'rational basis' exists for so concluding." *Ibid.* (quoting *United States v. Lopez*, 514 U.S. 549, 557 (1995)). In addition, by virtue of the Necessary and Proper Clause, Art. I, § 8, Cl. 18, "the Constitution's grants of specific federal legislative authority are accompanied by broad power to enact laws that are 'convenient, or useful' or 'conducive' to the authority's 'beneficial exercise.'" *United States v. Comstock*, 130 S. Ct. 1949, 1956 (2010) (quoting *McCulloch v. Maryland*, 17 U.S. (4 Wheat.) 316, 413, 418 (1819)). These principles reinforce the "presumption of constitutionality" this Court applies "when examining the scope of Congressional power." *Id.* at 1957 (quoting *United States v. Morrison*, 529 U.S. 598, 607 (2000)).

The minimum coverage provision is a valid exercise of Congress's Commerce power. It prescribes a rule that governs the manner in which individuals finance their participation in the health care market, and it does so through the predominant means of financing in that market—insurance. It directly addresses the consequences of economic conduct that distorts the interstate markets for health care and health insurance—namely the attempt by millions of Americans to self-insure or rely on the back-stop of free care, and the billions of dollars in cost-shifting that conduct produces each year when the uninsured do not pay for the care they inevitably need and receive. See *Lopez*, 514 U.S. at 560 ("Where economic activity substantially affects interstate commerce, legislation regulating that activity will be sustained."). And it is necessary to make effective the insurance market reforms (guaranteed issue and community rating) that all agree Congress has the authority to impose.

Congress's enactment of the minimum coverage provision thus rests upon direct, tangible, and well-documented economic effects on interstate commerce (reflected in specific congressional findings), not effects "so indirect and remote that to embrace them * * * would effectually obliterate the distinction between what is national and what is local." *Lopez*, 514 U.S. at 556-557 (quoting *NLRB v. Jones & Laughlin Steel Corp.*, 301 U.S. 1, 37 (1937)). As Judge Sutton recognized, "[n]o one must 'pile inference upon inference,' *Lopez*, 514 U.S. at 567, to recognize that the national regulation of a $2.5 trillion industry, much of it financed through 'health insurance . . . sold by national or regional health insurance companies,' 42 U.S.C. 18091(a)(2)(B), is economic in nature." *Thomas More*, 2011 WL 2556039, at *25 (Sutton, J., concurring in the judgment). The provision does not intrude on the sovereignty of the States; it regulates private conduct, operating on individuals, not States. Cf. *Printz v. United States*, 521 U.S. 898, 904- 933 (1997). It addresses a problem individual States have had difficulty solving on their own in the absence of a nationally uniform insurance requirement. App. 231a (Marcus, J., dissenting); see *Hodel v. Virginia Surface Mining & Reclamation Ass'n, Inc.*, 452 U.S. 264, 281- 282 (1981). It is an integral part of a comprehensive regulatory scheme that the Commerce power plainly authorizes Congress to enact. *Raich*, 545 U.S. at 15-22. And it violates no other substantive constitutional limitation.

Indeed, the court of appeals, like respondents, did not dispute that the Constitution provides Congress with the authority to pursue the ends the minimum coverage provision seeks to achieve. The objection was to the particular means Congress has chosen—the decision to prescribe a general insurance requirement rather than regulating "at the point of consumption" by denying care to (or imposing a financial penalty on) individuals without insurance. App. 118a; App. 207a (Marcus, J., dissenting). But respondents have identified nothing in this Court's precedents that would deny Congress the authority to effectuate its objectives through the means of a minimum coverage provision, one that is appropriate and plainly adapted to Congress's concededly legitimate ends. See *McCulloch*, 17 U.S. (4 Wheat.) at 421. As this Court has repeatedly held, the Constitution "'addresse[s]' the 'choice of means' 'primarily . . . to the judgment of Congress.'" *Comstock*, 130 S. Ct. at 1957 (brackets in original) (quoting Burroughs v. United States, 290 U.S. 534, 547-548 (1934)); see also *Raich*, 545 U.S. at 36 (Scalia, J., concurring in the judgment) ("[W]here Congress has the authority to enact a regulation of interstate commerce, 'it possesses every power needed to make that regulation effective.'") (quoting *United States v. Wrightwood Dairy Co.,* 315 U.S. 110, 118-119 (1942)). Accordingly, there is no basis for concluding that the minimum coverage provision exceeds Congress's commerce power.

a. Participation in the health care market is virtually universal, and individuals (including the uninsured) are always at risk of needing unanticipated care. That participation may be paid for (and that risk covered) in one of two ways—either through insurance, or through attempted self-insurance with the back-stop of uncompensated care. *Thomas More,* 2011 WL 2556039, at *29 (Sutton, J., concurring in the judgment). The minimum coverage provision thus regulates the way participants in the health care market finance the services they consume. App. 213a-214a (Marcus, J., dissenting). And it does so in an entirely ordinary and appropriate way; because "health care costs are inevitable, unpredictable, and often staggeringly high," services in the health care market, "unlike other markets, [are] paid for predominantly through the mechanism of insurance." App. 246a (Marcus, J., dissenting); cf. *McCulloch,* 17 U.S. (4 Wheat.) at 409 ("[T]he powers given to the government imply the ordinary means of execution.").

Congress had far more than a rational basis for concluding that the economic conduct it was regulating had a substantial effect on interstate commerce. Individuals without insurance actively participate in the health care market, but they pay only a fraction of the cost of the services they consume. App. 193a-194a, 211a-213a (Marcus, J., dissenting). On average, the uninsured pay only 37% of their health care costs out of pocket, and third parties, such as government programs and charities, pay another 26% on their behalf. App. 193a (Marcus, J., dissenting). "The remaining costs are uncompensated— they are borne by health care providers and are passed on in the form of increased premiums to individuals who already participate in the insurance market." App. 193a-194a (Marcus, J., dissenting). In 2008, the uninsured consumed approximately $116 billion in health care services, including $43 billion worth of care for which the providers were not compensated. App. 194a, 212a (Marcus, J., dissenting) (citing 42 U.S.C.A. 18091(a)(2)(F)). Congress found that providers pass some of those costs on to insurers, which pass them on to insured consumers, raising average family premiums by $1000 in 2008. App. 194a (Marcus, J., dissenting) (citing 42 U.S.C.A. 18091(a)(2)(F)). "This cost shifting does not occur in other markets, even those in which we all participate." App. 251a (Marcus, J., dissenting).

b. Respondents contend that the minimum coverage provision is an impermissible means of addressing these substantial effects on interstate commerce because it regulates "inactivity," *e.g.*, States' C.A. Br. 20-21. No court of appeals has accepted that proposition, which lacks any foundation in the Constitution's text or this Court's precedents. See *Lopez*, 514 U.S. at 569-571 (Kennedy, J., concurring) (noting that the Court's commerce cases have rejected "semantic or formalistic categories" in favor of "broad principles of economic practicality"). As Judge Sutton explained in *Thomas More*, "[n]o one is inactive when deciding how to pay for health care, as self-insurance and private insurance are two forms of action for addressing the same risk." 2011 WL 2556039, at *29. Even the majority below was "not persuaded that the formalistic dichotomy of activity and inactivity provides a workable or persuasive enough answer in this case." App. 100a.

The court of appeals nevertheless invalidated the minimum coverage provision, based on a supposed constitutional rule about timing. The court explicitly recognized (and respondents expressly conceded below) that when the uninsured "consume health care, Congress may regulate their activity at the point of consumption." App. 118a; see App. 207a-208a (Marcus, J., dissenting). But the majority then went on to conclude that a requirement to obtain insurance could apply no earlier. App. 115a-119a. The majority thus essentially adopted the position urged by respondents, *i.e.*, that in lieu of the minimum coverage provision, Congress should have addressed the problem of cost-shifting in the interstate health care market by "imposing restrictions or penalties on individuals who attempt to consume health care services without insurance." App. 207a-208a (Marcus, J., dissenting) (quoting States C.A. Br. 31-32).[3]

The court of appeals' reasoning reflects both a serious departure from the appropriate deference due Congress in its choice of means and a basic misunderstanding of the way health insurance works. Even assuming that respondents or the court of appeals could identify a preferable regulatory alternative, that would provide no basis to invalidate the one that Congress chose. "The relevant question is simply whether the means chosen are 'reasonably adapted' to the attainment of a legitimate end under the commerce power." *Raich*,

545 U.S. at 37 (Scalia, J., concurring in the judgment) (citation omitted); see *McCulloch*, 17 U.S. (4 Wheat.) at 421 ("Let the end be legitimate, let it be within the scope of the constitution, and all means which are appropriate, which are plainly adapted to that end, which are not prohibited, but consist with the letter and spirit of the constitution, are constitutional.").

In *Thomas More*, Judge Sutton explained why the timing of the minimum coverage provision's application (which the court of appeals here viewed as dispositive) is in fact immaterial from a constitutional perspective. 2011 WL 2556039, at *30. "Requiring insurance today and requiring it at a future point of sale amount to policy differences in degree, not kind, and not the sort of policy differences removed from the political branches by the word 'proper' or for that matter 'necessary' or 'regulate' or 'commerce.'" *Ibid.* Moreover, respondents' preferred scheme "would impose a federal condition (ability to pay) on the consumption of a service bound up in federal commerce (medical care)." *Ibid.* Such a condition "would be at least as coercive as the individual mandate, and arguably more so." *Ibid.*

It has long been settled that the "exertion of federal power" under the Commerce Clause need not "await the disruption of * * * commerce." *Consolidated Edison Co. v. NLRB*, 305 U.S. 197, 222 (1938). Instead, "Congress [is] entitled to provide reasonable preventive measures." *Ibid.* The Court applied that principle in *Raich*. Like respondents here, the plaintiff in that case (a grower of homegrown marijuana for personal medical consumption) claimed that Congress could not regulate her because she was "entirely separated from the market." 545 U.S. at 30 (citation omitted). The

Court rejected that artificial limit on Congress's commerce power, see id. at 25-33, because "marijuana that is grown at home and possessed for personal use is never more than an instant from the interstate market," *id.* at 40 (Scalia, J., concurring in the judgment). The same principle applies here. Because of human susceptibility to disease and accident, we are all "never more than an instant" (*ibid.*) from the "point of consumption" of health care (App. 118a). Nothing in the Commerce Clause requires Congress to withhold federal regulation until that moment. App. 210a (Marcus, J., dissenting) (Commerce Clause does not "requir[e] Congress to wait until the cost-shifting problem materializes for each uninsured person before it may regulate the uninsured as a class."); see *Liberty University, Inc. v. Geithner*, No. 10-2347, 2011 WL 3962915, at *41 (4th Cir. Sept. 8, 2011) (Davis, J., dissenting) (*Liberty University*).

Indeed, the court of appeals' focus on the point of "consumption" disregards the economic rationale for insurance, which, by its nature, must be obtained before medical care is needed. "Health insurance is a mechanism for spreading the costs of that medical care across people or over time, from a period when the cost would be overwhelming to periods when costs are more manageable." App. 197a (Marcus, J., dissenting) (quoting C.A. Econ. Scholars Amicus Br. Supporting the Federal Government 12). Common sense, experience, and economic analysis show that a "health insurance market could never survive or even form if people could buy their insurance on the way to the hospital." *47 Million and Counting: Why the Health Care Marketplace Is Broken: Hearing Before the S. Comm. on Finance*, 110th Cong., 2d Sess. 52 (2008) (Prof. Mark A. Hall).

The court of appeals' exclusive focus on the point of future consumption also ignores the reality that insurance rates are calculated on the basis of the present risk that such future expenses will occur. The risk of substantial medical expenses is universal, and few who attempt to self-insure can come close to covering the full expenses they would incur if the risk were to materialize. As a result, the present premiums others pay must cover the risk of the uninsured. The uninsured thus externalize the cost of their present medical risk to others every day, not at some indeterminate future time, and they similarly externalize the cost of maintaining the medical infrastructure that will be available to them when needed. The minimum coverage provision simply ensures that individuals who can afford insurance (and are otherwise non-exempted) will pay for the health care services they consume and the risks to which they are exposed, rather than shift those costs and risks to others, now and in the future. See *Thomas More*, 2011 WL 2556039, at *24 (Sutton, J., concurring in the judgment) ("Faced with $43 billion in uncompensated care, Congress reasonably could require all covered individuals to pay for health care now so that money would be available later to pay for *all* care as the need arises.").

The fact that some of the uninsured may not generate uncompensated costs in a particular month or year provides no basis for invalidating the statute. "When Congress decides that the 'total incidence' of a practice poses a threat to a national market, it may regulate the entire class." *Raich*, 545 U.S. at 17 (quoting *Perez v. United States*, 402 U.S. 146, 154 (1971)). Accordingly, Congress was not required to predict, person-by-person, who among the uninsured will receive uncompensated medical services in a given month or year, and it would be infeasible to do so. App. 215a (Marcus, J., dissenting). It is, rather, the very nature of insurance—the customary means of financing health care—to address such risks in the aggregate.

    c. Instead of deferring to Congress's policy judgments, the court of appeals majority made its own independent judgment that the minimum coverage provision will not adequately accomplish Congress's objective of reducing cost-shifting because of its exemptions and enforcement mechanisms. App. 151a-152a. That analysis "looks startlingly like strict scrutiny review," App. 218a (Marcus, J., dissenting), even though "[t]he courts do not apply strict scrutiny to commerce clause legislation and require only an 'appropriate' or 'reasonable' 'fit' between means and ends," *Thomas More*, 2011 WL 2556039, at *31 (Sutton, J., concurring in the judgment).

    Based on an extensive legislative record, Congress reasonably concluded that the minimum coverage provision will mitigate the problem of cost-shifting in the health care market. Indeed, the CBO has estimated that, without the minimum coverage provision, there would be 16 million more people without insurance in 2019. *Eliminating the Individual Mandate* 2; see Matthew Buettgens, et al., Urban Inst., *Why the Individual Mandate Matters* 1 (Dec. 2010) (concluding that uncompensated care would decline by only $14.7 billion if the Act contained no minimum coverage provision). At the very least, the CBO's analysis demonstrates that Congress's determination that the minimum coverage provision will effectively reduce the number of uninsured individuals was reasonable. The court of appeals should not have substituted its judgment for that of Congress. See *Thomas More*, 2011 WL 2556039, at *33 (Sutton, J., concurring in the judgment)

("Time assuredly will bring to light the policy strengths and weaknesses of using the [minimum coverage provision] as part of this national legislation, allowing the peoples' political representatives, rather than their judges, to have the primary say over its utility."); see also *Preseault v. ICC*, 494 U.S. 1, 18-19 (1990).

    d. The minimum coverage provision is also "necessary and proper for the regulation of interstate commerce"—and distinguishable from the statutes in *Lopez* and *Morrison*—because it is "an essential part of a larger regulation of economic activity, in which the regulatory scheme could be undercut unless the intrastate activity were regulated." *Raich*, 545 U.S. at 36 (Scalia, J., concurring in the judgment) (quoting *Lopez*, 514 U.S. at 561); see App. 229a-232a (Marcus, J. dissenting); *Thomas More*, 2011 WL 2556039, at *12-*14 (Martin, J.). "Health care and the means of paying for it are 'quintessentially economic' in a way that possessing guns near schools and domestic violence are not." *Id.* at *25 (Sutton, J., concurring in the judgment) (*citing Lopez, supra*, and *Morrison, supra*). Moreover, Congress found that the minimum coverage provision was "essential" to the success of the measures it adopted to end insurance discrimination against those with pre-existing conditions. 42 U.S.C.A. 18091(a)(2)(I). Those insurance reforms are unquestionably within Congress's powers under the Commerce Clause. See *United States v. South-Eastern Underwriters Ass'n*, 322 U.S. 533, 539-553 (1944). The soundness of Congress's judgment about what was required for its insurance reforms to succeed is supported by the experience of States that tried—and failed—to effectively end such practices without an insurance requirement. See App. 230a-231a (Marcus, J., dissenting). Indeed, no party to this case has suggested that the guaranteed-issue and community-rating requirements could function effectively without the minimum coverage provision.

The court of appeals thought that the minimum coverage provision could not be upheld as an essential part of a larger regulatory program because that constitutional rationale is inapplicable to "facial" challenges, such as the one at issue in this case and in *Lopez.* App. 144a-145a. *Lopez* itself, however, suggested just the opposite. "Though the conduct in *Lopez* was not economic, the Court neverthe-less recognized that it could be regulated as 'an essential part of a larger regulatory activity, in which the regulatory scheme could be undercut unless the intrastate activity was regulated.'" *Raich,* 545 U.S. at 36 (Scalia, J., concurring in the judgment) (quoting *Lopez,* 514 U.S. at 561). The court of appeals also stated that *Raich* was "the only instance in which a statute has been sustained by the larger regulatory scheme doctrine," and it perceived that the doctrine was limited to that case's facts, *i.e.,* when "Congress [seeks] to eliminate *all* interstate traffic in [a] commodity." App. 146a. That is doubly incorrect. The Court relied on this doctrine to uphold statutes well before *Raich,* and it did so in a variety of regulatory contexts not involving the prohibition of trade in a commodity. See, e.g., 545 U.S. at 37-38 (Scalia, J., concurring in the judgment) (discussing *United States v. Darby,* 312 U.S. 100, 125 (1941)); *Hodel v. Indiana,* 452 U.S. 314, 329 n.17 (1981).

2. CONGRESS'S TAXING POWER PROVIDES INDEPENDENT AUTHORITY FOR THE ENACTMENT OF THE MINIMUM COVERAGE PROVISION

Congress's constitutional power "[t]o lay and collect Taxes, Duties, Imposts and Excises," Art. I, § 8, Cl. 1, provides an independent basis to uphold the Act's minimum coverage provision. The taxing power is "comprehensive," *Steward Mach. Co. v. Davis*, 301 U.S. 548, 581-582 (1937), and, in "passing on the constitutionality of a tax law," a court is "concerned only with its practical operation, not its definition or the precise form of descriptive words which may be applied to it." *Nelson v. Sears, Roebuck & Co.*, 312 U.S. 359, 363 (1941) (quoting *Lawrence v. State Tax Comm'n*, 286 U.S. 276, 280 (1932)).

The "practical operation" of the minimum coverage provision is as a tax. *Nelson*, 312 U.S. at 363; accord *Liberty University*, 2011 WL 3962915, at *16-*22 (Wynn, J., concurring). The provision amends the Internal Revenue Code to provide that a non-exempted individual who fails to maintain a minimum level of coverage shall pay a tax penalty for each month that he fails to maintain that coverage. 26 U.S.C.A. 5000A. The amount of the penalty is calculated as a percentage of household income for federal income tax purposes, subject to a floor and a cap. 26 U.S.C.A. 5000A(c). The penalty is reported on the individual's federal income tax return for the taxable year, and is "assessed and collected in the same manner as" other assessable tax penalties under the Internal Revenue Code. 26 U.S.C.A. 5000A(b)(2) and (g). Individuals who are not required to file income tax returns for a given year are not required to pay the penalty. 26 U.S.C.A. 5000A(e)(2). A taxpayer's responsibility for family members depends on their status as dependents under the Internal Revenue Code. 26 U.S.C.A. 5000A(a) and (b)(3). Taxpayers filing a joint tax return are jointly liable for the penalty. 26 U.S.C.A. 5000A(b)(3)(B). And the Secretary of the Treasury is empowered to enforce the penalty provision. 26 U.S.C.A. 5000A(g).

It is undisputed that the minimum coverage provision will be "productive of some revenue." *Sonzinsky v. United States*, 300 U.S. 506, 514 (1937). The CBO found that it will raise at least $4 billion a year in revenues for the general treasury. See Letter from Douglas Elmendorf, Director, CBO, to Nancy Pelosi, Speaker, House of Reps., Tbl. 4 (Mar. 20, 2010). The provision unquestionably bears "some reasonable relation" to the "raising of revenue," *United States v. Doremus*, 249 U.S. 86, 93-94 (1919), and it is therefore within Congress's taxing power.

This conclusion is reinforced by examining the broader statutory context. The minimum coverage provision is just one of numerous ways in which the Affordable Care Act amends the Internal Revenue Code to expand insurance coverage. The Act will provide tax credits for many individuals who purchase coverage through an exchange, see 26 U.S.C.A. 36B, and for eligible small businesses that provide coverage to their employees, 26 U.S.C.A. 45R. Under certain circumstances, it also provides for tax penalties for large employers that do not offer adequate coverage to full-time employees. 26 U.S.C.A. 4980H. Those provisions in turn build upon numerous pre-existing provisions of the Internal Revenue Code related to health insurance coverage. Each of those measures is unquestionably a proper exercise of the taxing power, and, in their practical effect, they are equivalent to the minimum coverage provision—they all use the tax code to provide financial incentives that favor health insurance coverage.[4]

Indeed, just as deductions, exemptions, and credits operate to reduce a taxpayer's income tax liability based on the individual circumstances of the taxpayer, the minimum coverage penalty simply has the effect of increasing the taxpayer's total liability on his income tax return based on his own individual circumstances. In its practical operation, the minimum coverage provision is thus the mirror image of statutory provisions of the sort that have long been regarded as within Congress's broad discretion to determine the amount of tax owed, and falls equally within Congress's broad taxing power.

The court of appeals concluded that Congress did not intend to exercise its taxing power in enacting the minimum coverage provision because it referred to the assessment as a "penalty." App. 157a-172a; accord *Thomas More*, 2011 WL 3692915, at *17-*21. There is no such magic words test. See *Liberty University*, 2011 WL 3962915, at *17 (Wynn, J., concurring); see also *United States v. Sotelo*, 436 U.S. 268, 275 (1978) (funds owed by operation of Internal Revenue Code had "essential character as taxes" despite statutory label as "penalt[ies]"); *Nelson*, 312 U.S. at 363. Moreover, if Section 5000A can reasonably be interpreted as a valid exercise of the tax power—and it surely can be because it is fully integrated into the Internal Revenue Code, and is an adjunct to the income tax—then the courts must adopt that interpretation, even if other interpretations of congressional intent are also reasonable. See *Edward J. DeBartolo Corp. v. Florida Gulf Coast Bldg. & Constr. Trades Council*, 485 U.S. 568, 575 (1988).

The court of appeals noted that the goal of the minimum coverage provision is not to raise revenue, but to reduce the number of people who are uninsured. App. 164a. It is settled, however, that a tax "does not cease to be valid merely because it regulates, discourages, or even definitely deters the activities taxed." *United States v. Sanchez*, 340 U.S. 42, 44 (1950); see *Liberty University*, 2011 WL 3962916, at *17-*18 (Wynn, J., concurring). "Every tax is in some measure regulatory" in that "it interposes an economic impediment to the activity taxed as compared with others not taxed." *Sonzinsky*, 300 U.S. at 513. So long as a statute is "productive of some revenue," Congress may exercise its taxing powers irrespective of any "collateral inquiry as to the measure of the regulatory effect of a tax." *Id*. at 514.

3. THE COURT OF APPEALS' DECISION CONFLICTS WITH A DECISION OF THE SIXTH CIRCUIT AND INVOLVES A QUESTION OF FUNDAMENTAL IMPORTANCE

The court of appeals' conclusion that the minimum coverage provision exceeds Congress's power under the Commerce Clause conflicts with a contrary holding of the Sixth Circuit. See *Thomas More*, 2011 WL 2556039, at *1.[5] Although the Sixth Circuit issued its decision approximately six weeks before the court of appeals' decision in this case, the majority here did not mention the Sixth Circuit's contrary view, much less respond to it.

Writing for himself in *Thomas More*, Judge Martin concluded that "the minimum coverage provision is facially constitutional under the Commerce Clause" because it regulates economic activity—"the financing of health care services, and specifically the practice of self insuring for the cost of care"—with a substantial effect on interstate commerce—"driving up the cost of health care as well as * * * shifting costs to third parties." 2011 WL 2556039, at *11-*12. Judge Martin further concluded that "even if self-insuring for the cost of health care were not economic activity with a substantial effect on interstate commerce, Congress could still properly regulate the practice because the failure to do so would undercut its regulation of the larger interstate markets in health care delivery and health insurance." *Id.* at *12.

Judge Sutton, concurring in the judgment, concluded that the minimum coverage provision regulates the practice of self-insurance against health risk and observed that "[t]here are two ways to self-insure, and both, when aggregated, substantially affect interstate commerce." *Thomas More*, 2011 WL 2556039, at *24. "One option is to save money so that it is there when the need for health care arises. The other is to save nothing and to rely on something else—good fortune or the good graces of others—when the need arises." *Ibid.* In his view, "Congress reasonably could require *all* covered individuals to pay for health care now so that money would be available later to pay for *all* care as the need arises." *Ibid*.

Judge Sutton also rejected the contention that "the Commerce Clause contain[s] an action/inaction dichotomy that limits congressional power" but, in any event, found the distinction immaterial in this context because "[n]o one is inactive when deciding how to pay for health care, as self-insurance and private insurance are two forms of action for addressing the same risk. Each requires affirmative choices; one is no less active than the other." *Thomas More*, 2011 WL 2556039, at *27, *29. In sum, Judge Sutton concluded that "[i]f Congress has the power to regulate the national healthcare market, as all seem to agree, it is difficult to see why it lacks authority to regulate a unique feature of that market by requiring all to pay now in affordable premiums for what virtually none can pay later in the form of, say, $100,000 (or more) of medical bills prompted by a medical emergency." *Id*. at *30.

This Court's review is warranted to resolve the conflict in the circuits.6 Review is especially appropriate because the court of appeals "str[uck] down as unconstitutional a central piece of a comprehensive economic regulatory scheme enacted by Congress" to address a matter of grave national importance. App. 189a (Marcus, J., dissenting).

B. THE COURT SHOULD ADDRESS WHETHER THE ANTI-INJUNCTION ACT BARS THIS PRE-ENFORCEMENT CHALLENGE TO THE MINIMUM COVERAGE PROVISION WE RESPECTFULLY SUGGEST THAT THE COURT DIRECT THE PARTIES TO ADDRESS THE APPLICABILITY OF THE ANTIINJUNCTION ACT, 26 U.S.C. 7421(A), TO RESPONDENTS' CHALLENGE TO THE MINIMUM COVERAGE PROVISION.

Subject to certain exceptions, the Anti-Injunction Act provides that "no suit for the purpose of restraining the assessment or collection of any tax shall be maintained in any court by any person, whether or not such person is the person against whom such tax was assessed." *Ibid.*

In the district court, the federal government moved to dismiss respondents' challenge to the minimum coverage provision on the ground that the Anti-Injunction Act barred it. The district court declined to dismiss on that basis, see App. 401a-425a, and the federal government did not challenge that ruling on appeal. In a supplemental brief requested by the Fourth Circuit, the federal government explained that it had reconsidered its position on this question and had "concluded that the [AntiInjunction Act] does not fore-close the exercise of jurisdiction in these cases." Fed. Gov't Supplemental Br. at 2, *Liberty University, supra* (No. 10-2347).

The government also set out the legal basis for its position that the Anti-Injunction Act does not apply. See *id.* at 2-9.

The court of appeals in this case did not address the Anti-Injunction Act, but in two other cases circuit courts did so, reaching conflicting results. In *Thomas More*, the Sixth Circuit, consistent with the position of the United States on appeal in that case, unanimously held that "the Anti-Injunction Act d[id] not remove [its] juris-diction to consider this claim." 2011 WL 2556039, at *8. In *Liberty University*, however, a divided panel of the Fourth Circuit held that the challenge before it was barred by the Anti-Injunction Act. See 2011 WL 3962915, at *4-*16.

The United States continues to believe that the AntiInjunction Act does not bar these challenges to the minimum coverage provision. But the courts of appeals are now divided on the question. This Court has stated that "the object of [the Anti-Injunction Act] is to withdraw jurisdiction from the state and federal courts." *Enochs v. Williams Packing & Navigation Co.,* 370 U.S. 1, 5 (1962); see *Bob Jones Univ. v. Simon*, 416 U.S. 725, 749 (1974); but cf. *Helvering v. Davis*, 301 U.S. 619, 639-640 (1937) (accepting express waiver of Anti-Injunction Act by the United States). Under these circumstances, we believe the Court should consider the applicability of the Anti-Injunction Act along with the constitutional issues in this case. If, as we antici-pate, respondents take the position that the Anti-Injunction Act does not bar this suit, the Court should also consider appointing an amicus to file a brief defending the position that the AntiInjunction Act does bar this suit, as the majority held in Liberty University. In the event the Court finds the Anti-Injunction Act inapplicable, it can then decide the constitutional questions.

1. What is the crux of this case? What is self-insurance, and why do some individuals want to self-insure?

2. What was the court's decision, and what does this tell us about the health care market?

NATIONAL FEDERATION OF INDEPENDENT BUSINESS V. SEBELIUS 567 U.S. 519 (2012), FROM THE US SUPREME COURT, JUNE 28, 2012

In 2010, Congress enacted the Patient Protection and Affordable Care Act in order to increase the number of Americans covered by health insurance and decrease the cost of health care. One key provision is the individual mandate, which requires most Americans to maintain "minimum essential" health insurance coverage. 26 U. S. C. §5000A. For individuals who are not exempt, and who do not receive health insurance through an employer or government program, the means of satisfying the requirement is to purchase insurance from a private company. Beginning in 2014, those who do not comply with the mandate must make a "[s]hared responsibility payment" to the Federal Government. §5000A(b)(1). The Act provides that this "penalty" will be paid to the Internal Revenue Service with an individual's taxes, and "shall be assessed and collected in the same manner" as tax penalties. §§5000A(c), (g)(1).

Another key provision of the Act is the Medicaid expansion. The current Medicaid program offers federal funding to States to assist pregnant women, children, needy families, the blind, the elderly, and the disabled in obtaining medical care. 42 U. S. C. §1396d(a). The Affordable Care Act expands the scope of the Medicaid program and increases the number of individuals the States must cover. For example, the Act requires state programs to provide Medicaid coverage by 2014 to adults with incomes up to 133 percent of the federal poverty level, whereas many States now cover adults with children only if their income is considerably lower, and do not cover childless adults at all. §1396a(a)(10)(A)(i)(VIII). The Act increases federal funding to cover the States' costs in expanding Medicaid coverage. §1396d(y)(1). But if a State does not comply with the Act's new coverage requirements, it may lose not only the federal funding for those requirements, but all of its federal Medicaid funds. §1396c.

Twenty-six States, several individuals, and the National Federation of Independent Business brought suit in Federal District Court, challenging the constitutionality of the individual mandate and the Medicaid expansion. The Court of Appeals for the Eleventh Circuit upheld the Medicaid expansion as a valid exercise of Congress's spending power, but concluded that Congress lacked authority to enact the individual mandate. Finding the mandate severable from the Act's other provisions, the Eleventh Circuit left the rest of the Act intact.

Held: The judgment is affirmed in part and reversed in part.

648 F. 3d 1235, affirmed in part and reversed in part.

1. Chief Justice Roberts delivered the opinion of the Court with respect to Part II, concluding that the Anti-Injunction Act does not bar this suit.

The Anti-Injunction Act provides that "no suit for the purpose of restraining the assessment or collection of any tax shall be maintained in any court by any person," 26 U. S. C. §7421(a), so that those subject to a tax must first pay it and then sue for a refund. The present challenge seeks to restrain the collection of the shared responsibility payment from those who do not comply with the individual mandate. But Congress did not intend the payment to be treated as a "tax" for purposes of the Anti-Injunction Act. The Affordable Care Act describes the payment as a "penalty," not a "tax." That label cannot control whether the payment is a tax for purposes of the Constitution, but it does determine the application of the Anti-Injunction Act. The Anti-Injunction Act therefore does not bar this suit. Pp. 11–15.

2. Chief Justice Roberts concluded in Part III–A that the individual mandate is not a valid exercise of Congress's power under the Commerce Clause and the Necessary and Proper Clause. Pp. 16–30.

(a) The Constitution grants Congress the power to "*regulate* Commerce." Art. I, §8, cl. 3 (emphasis added). The power to regulate commerce presupposes the existence of commercial activity to be regulated. This Court's precedent reflects this understanding: As expansive as this Court's cases construing the scope of the commerce power have been, they uniformly describe the power as reaching "activity." *E.g., United States v. Lopez*, 514 U. S. 549 . The individual mandate, however, does not regulate existing commercial activity. It instead compels individuals to become active in commerce by purchasing a product, on the ground that their failure to do so affects interstate commerce.

Construing the Commerce Clause to permit Congress to regulate individuals precisely *because* they are doing nothing would open a new and potentially vast domain to congressional authority. Congress already possesses expansive power to regulate what people do. Upholding the Affordable Care Act under the Commerce Clause would give Congress the same license to regulate what people do not do. The Framers knew the difference between doing something and doing nothing. They gave Congress the power to *regulate* commerce, not to *compel* it. Ignoring that distinction would undermine the principle that the Federal Government is a government of limited and enumerated powers. The individual mandate thus cannot be sustained under Congress's power to "regulate Commerce." Pp. 16–27.

(b) Nor can the individual mandate be sustained under the Necessary and Proper Clause as an integral part of the Affordable Care Act's other reforms. Each of this Court's prior cases upholding laws under that Clause involved exercises of authority derivative of, and in service to, a granted power. E.g., *United States v. Comstock*, 560 U. S. ___. The individual mandate, by contrast, vests Congress with the extraordinary ability to create the necessary predicate to the exercise of an enumerated power and draw within its regulatory scope those who would otherwise be outside of it. Even if the individual mandate is "necessary" to the Affordable Care Act's other reforms, such an expansion of federal power is not a "proper" means for making those reforms effective. Pp. 27–30.

3. Chief Justice Roberts concluded in Part III–B that the individual mandate must be construed as imposing a tax on those who do not have health insurance, if such a construction is reasonable.

The most straightforward reading of the individual mandate is that it commands individuals to purchase insurance. But, for the reasons explained, the Commerce Clause does not give Congress that power. It is therefore necessary to turn to the Government's alternative argument: that the mandate may be upheld as within Congress's power to "lay and collect Taxes." Art. I, §8, cl. 1. In pressing its taxing power argument, the Government asks the Court to view the mandate as imposing a tax on those who do not buy that product. Because "every reasonable construction must be resorted to, in order to save a statute from unconstitutionality," *Hooper v. California*, 155 U. S. 648 , the question is whether it is "fairly possible" to interpret the mandate as imposing such a tax, *Crowell v. Benson*, 285 U. S. 22 . Pp. 31–32.

4. Chief Justice Roberts delivered the opinion of the Court with respect to Part III–C, concluding that the individual mandate may be upheld as within Congress's power under the Taxing Clause. Pp. 33–44.

(a) The Affordable Care Act describes the "[s]hared responsibility payment" as a "penalty," not a "tax." That label is fatal to the application of the Anti-Injunction Act. It does not, however, control whether an exaction is within Congress's power to tax. In answering that constitutional question, this Court follows a functional approach, "[d]isregarding the designation of the exaction, and viewing its substance and application." *United States v. Constantine*, 296 U. S. 287 . Pp. 33–35.

(b) Such an analysis suggests that the shared responsibility payment may for constitutional purposes be considered a tax. The payment is not so high that there is really no choice but to buy health insurance; the payment is not limited to willful violations, as penalties for unlawful acts often are; and the payment is collected solely by the IRS through the normal means of taxation. Cf. *Bailey v. Drexel Furniture Co.*, 259 U. S. 20 –37. None of this is to say that payment is not intended to induce the purchase of health insurance. But the mandate need not be read to declare that failing to do so is unlawful. Neither the Affordable Care Act nor any other law attaches negative legal consequences to not buying health insurance, beyond requiring a payment to the IRS. And Congress's choice of language—stating that individuals "shall" obtain insurance or pay a "penalty"—does not require reading §5000A as punishing unlawful conduct. It may also be read as imposing a tax on those who go without insurance. See *New York v. United States,* 505 U. S. 144 –174. Pp. 35–40.

(c) Even if the mandate may reasonably be characterized as a tax, it must still comply with the Direct Tax Clause, which provides: "No Capitation, or other direct, Tax shall be laid, unless in Proportion to the Census or Enumeration herein before directed to be taken." Art. I, §9, cl. 4. A tax on going without health insurance is not like a capitation or other direct tax under this Court's precedents. It therefore need not be apportioned so that each State pays in proportion to its population. Pp. 40–41.

5. Chief Justice Roberts, joined by Justice Breyer and Justice Kagan, concluded in Part IV that the Medicaid expansion violates the Constitution by threatening States

with the loss of their existing Medicaid funding if they decline to comply with the expansion. Pp. 45–58.

(a) The Spending Clause grants Congress the power "to pay the Debts and provide for the . . . general Welfare of the United States." Art. I, §8, cl. 1. Congress may use this power to establish cooperative state-federal Spending Clause programs. The legitimacy of Spending Clause legislation, however, depends on whether a State voluntarily and knowingly accepts the terms of such programs. *Pennhurst State School* and *Hospital v. Halderman*, 451 U. S. 1 . "[T]he Constitution simply does not give Congress the authority to require the States to regulate." *New York v. United States*, 505 U. S. 144 . When Congress threatens to terminate other grants as a means of pressuring the States to accept a Spending Clause program, the legislation runs counter to this Nation's system of federalism. Cf. *South Dakota v. Dole*, 483 U. S. 203 . Pp. 45–51.

(b) Section 1396c gives the Secretary of Health and Human Services the authority to penalize States that choose not to participate in the Medicaid expansion by taking away their existing Medicaid funding. 42 U. S. C. §1396c. The threatened loss of over 10 percent of a State's overall budget is economic dragooning that leaves the States with no real option but to acquiesce in the Medicaid expansion. The Government claims that the expansion is properly viewed as only a modification of the existing program, and that this modification is permissible because Congress reserved the "right to alter, amend, or repeal any provision" of Medicaid. §1304. But the expansion accomplishes a shift in kind, not merely degree. The original program was designed to cover medical services for particular categories of vulnerable individuals. Under the Affordable Care Act, Medicaid is transformed into a program to meet the health care needs of the entire nonelderly population with income below 133 percent of the poverty level. A State could hardly anticipate that Congress's reservation of the right to "alter" or "amend" the Medicaid program included the power to transform it so dramatically. The Medicaid expansion thus violates the Constitution by threatening States with the loss of their existing Medicaid funding if they decline to comply with the expansion. Pp. 51–55.

(c) The constitutional violation is fully remedied by precluding the Secretary from applying §1396c to withdraw existing Medicaid funds for failure to comply with the requirements set out in the expansion. See §1303. The other provisions of the Affordable Care Act are not affected. Congress would have wanted the rest of the Act to stand, had it known that States would have a genuine choice whether to participate in the Medicaid expansion. Pp. 55–58

6. Justice Ginsburg, joined by Justice Sotomayor, is of the view that the Spending Clause does not preclude the Secretary from withholding Medicaid funds based on a State's refusal to comply with the expanded Medicaid program. But given the majority view, she agrees with The Chief Justice's conclusion in Part IV–B that the Medicaid Act's severability clause, 42 U. S. C. §1303, determines the appropriate remedy. Because The Chief Justice finds the withholding—not the granting—of federal funds incompatible with the Spending Clause, Congress' extension of Medicaid remains available to any State that affirms its willingness to participate. Even absent §1303's command, the Court would have no warrant to invalidate the funding offered by the Medicaid expansion, and surely no basis to

tear down the ACA in its entirety. When a court confronts an unconstitutional statute, its endeavor must be to conserve, not destroy, the legislation. See, e.g., *Ayotte v. Planned Parenthood of Northern New Eng.*, 546 U. S. 320 –330. Pp. 60–61.

Roberts, C. J., announced the judgment of the Court and delivered the opinion of the Court with respect to Parts I, II, and III–C, in which Ginsburg, Breyer, Sotomayor, and Kagan, JJ., joined; an opinion with respect to Part IV, in which Breyer and Kagan, JJ., joined; and an opinion with respect to Parts III–A, III–B, and III–D. Ginsburg, J., filed an opinion concurring in part, concurring in the judgment in part, and dissenting in part, in which Sotomayor, J., joined, and in which Breyer and Kagan, JJ., joined as to Parts I, II, III, and IV. Scalia, Kennedy, Thomas, and Alito, JJ., filed a dissenting opinion. Thomas, J., filed a dissenting opinion.

1. According to Chief Justice Roberts, why is the individual mandate constitutional? Which parts of the Constitution does he cite as evidence?

CHAPTER 4

WHAT ADVOCACY ORGANIZATIONS SAY

Advocacy organizations hold a very important place in the debate about health care. Organizations representing health care users, doctors, insurance companies, and pharmaceutical companies are just a few that have been vocal opponents or supporters of policy measures. Others work to influence policy while ensuring access through funding initiatives or awareness campaigns. But as with any high-controversy debate, advocacy groups need to be understood within their own context, specifically what policy they support and how they align themselves within the health care system. These facts, and others, can influence the kind of information they share, the way they frame the health care debate, and other facets of their work. That being said, advocacy groups are crucial for pushing the debate forward, and cannot be dismissed when talking about health care.

"MEDICARE FOR ALL ADVOCATES RIP 'CYNICAL AND DISHONEST' HEALTHCARE INITIATIVE AS PLOY AT UNDERMINE SINGLE PAYER," BY JULIA CONLEY, FROM *COMMON DREAMS*, FEBRUARY 7, 2018

"THE PATH ALREADY EXISTS. THE MOVEMENT ALREADY EXSTS. THE POLITICAL WILL EXISTS. WHAT'S LACKING IS A WILLINGNESS TO STAND UP FOR VALUES THAT PEOPLE ALREADY AGREE WITH FOR FEAR OF ALIENATING PEOPLE LIKE BILL FRIST."

Medicare for All advocates on Wednesday denounced a new healthcare initiative introduced by a bipartisan group of former lawmakers, health policy administrators, and healthcare sector CEOs.

Critics argue that the non-profit, United States of Care, ignores the majority of Americans who back government-run healthcare for all, instead catering to centrist Democrats in Washington who pledge to "ensure that every single American has access to quality, affordable healthcare" while insisting that a universal healthcare program—like the ones that exist in every other industrialized country in the world—is unfeasible.

The group, whose co-founders include former Sen. Bill Frist (R-Tenn.), who led efforts to privatize Medicare, is ambiguous about its plans for the American healthcare system, vaguely promising on its website to "change the conversation and put healthcare over politics."

But another co-founder of the new group, former Medicare and Medicaid administrator Andy Slavitt, has been clear about the group's opposition to a single-payer healthcare program.

"We believe every single American should have access to basic, affordable care," Slavitt told Modern Healthcare of the organization's mission. "But we avoid using language like 'universal coverage' that is polarizing."

In fact, single-payer healthcare has more public and political support than ever before, with 53 percent of Americans telling Kaiser Health Tracking, in a survey last year, that they supported a government-funded program.

Sen. Bernie Sanders' (I-Vt.) Medicare for All proposal has 16 co-sponsors, including several who are considered likely Democratic challengers to President Donald Trump in the 2020 presidential election.

The United States of Care puts forth three guiding principles for a healthcare plan for the U.S., writing that every American should be provided, an "affordable source of care," "protection from financial devastation," and a program with "political and economic viability."

"Of course, the left has a policy that ticks off all three boxes: Medicare for all," writes Matt Bruenig at the People's Policy Project. "Medicare for all achieves universal, affordable care. If you set the tax level at the right spot, it is 'fiscally responsible' and, because it basically annihilates the private insurance industry, it is almost impossible to undo later, meaning it is politically sustainable."

In a post on *Medium*, Katie Halper was one of several progressive critics who argued that the United States of Care has been specifically organized to stop single-payer healthcare from becoming a reality.

According to *Bloomberg*, "the organization is trying to prepare for an eventual opening for bipartisan policy making, while heading off increasingly volatile swings in health policy when political fortunes shift in Washington."

But if that interpretation is correct, warned Halper, "United States of Care exists to stop Single Payer in its tracks," not promote universal healthcare.

If that's the case, she continued, "this organization's very existence speaks to the strength, popularity and political viability of Medicare for All. And this would make its opposition to not pragmatic but ideological, cynical and dishonest, since one of the arguments against single payer is that it lacks a political mandate."

While the group insists that it's "building and mobilizing a movement to achieve long-lasting solutions that make health care better for everyone," critics on social media were among those arguing that the project ignores the reality of robust and growing support for Medicare for All.

For example, when former Obama speechwriter Jon Favreau claimed to be a "Medicare for All advocate," but complained there is no movement to "get there," he got immediately flayed by progressive critics.

"I would give you the benefit of the doubt," said another, "but you've been in politics long enough to know that you're [joking] us, Jon."

1. What role do advocacy groups like those described in this article play in the health care debate?

2. How would you summarize the stances of these two groups?

"ARIZONA ORGANIZATIONS URGE SENATE TO SAY NO TO NEW HEALTHCARE BILL," BY ALEXIS KUHBANDER AND KEVIN CUSACK, FROM *CRONKITE NEWS*, JUNE 27, 2017

PHOENIX — Arizona leaders of an array of organizations, ranging from AARP to Planned Parenthood, joined a chorus opposed to a Senate health care plan to replace the Affordable Care Act.

A news conference Tuesday at Chicanos Por La Causa drew attention to the Congressional Budget Office's estimate that the proposed plan would reduce the federal deficit faster than a House-proposed bill but cost 22 million people health care coverage.

They asked Arizona Senators John McCain and Jeff Flake to combat the bill, known as the American Health Care Act. Their plea came hours after Republican leader Mitch McConnell decided to delay discussion of the bill until senators return from July 4th recess.

President Donald Trump met with senators Tuesday evening to discuss the controversial bill. Republicans are divided over the proposal, with some saying it doesn't go far enough and others saying it cuts too much.

Republicans want to repeal the Affordable Care Act, known as Obamacare, as too expensive for taxpayers and hostile to insurance companies. McCain and others have said Obamacare amounts to federal overreach.

At Tuesday's conference in Arizona, representatives of organizations opposed to the measure included Planned Parenthood Advocates of Arizona, Organizing for Action, Lucha Arizona and AARP.

People living with HIV would be greatly affected, said Jonathan Brier, with the Aunt Rita's Foundation. He said cutting certain services proposed under the bill would be a death sentence.

Avondale Councilman Lorenzo Sierra said there is a face behind every fact uttered about health care in the U.S. His mother is one of them.

Sierra's mother died five years ago of cancer, two months after she was diagnosed. She worked at a minimum-wage job that did not provide her with health insurance, Sierra said.

"My mother had always been there for the state of Arizona and the United States in terms of being a workforce member," Sierra said. "When it came her time, America wasn't there for her, Arizona wasn't there for her. This bill won't be there for the millions and millions of people that are going to need it, like my mother."

1. Who might be most affected by changes to the ACA?

2. How might those most affected organize to fight against any proposed changes?

167

CHAPTER 5

WHAT THE MEDIA SAY

The media are crucial to providing the public with reliable information on all areas of public interest, including health care. But the media are also responsible for fact checking officials and other groups that seek to advocate for specific policies, and to provide context for the debate. Media coverage of health care features a great deal of fact-checking and reporting, and looking at the media landscape it is easy to find a range of voices that center varying elements of the health care conversation. Media coverage can give us a sense of the many factions in the debate, where they stand on differing policy positions, and how the debate on health care has evolved over time.

"CONTINUING SABOTAGE OF AMERICANS' HEALTHCARE, TRUMP PROPOSES ALLOWING INSURERS TO OFFER 'JUNK PLANS'," BY JESSICA CORBETT, FROM *COMMON DREAMS*, FEBRUARY 20, 2018

"WELCOME BACK TO: UNDERWRITING, DENIALS, HIGHER PREMIUMS FOR BEING SICK, AND POSSIBLY … INSUERS LEAING MARKETS. ALL OF THIS IS BY DESIGN."

The Trump administration is under fire for its latest move to sabotage the American healthcare system with an "unconscionable" proposed rule that would allow health insurance providers to offer what critics describe as "junk plans" that will drive up costs for patients and threaten necessary medical care for millions of Americans.

On Tuesday, in response to an executive order that President Donald Trump signed in October, Health and Human Services Secretary Alex Azar—in coordination with the Labor and Treasury departments—unveiled a proposal "to expand the availability of short-term, limited-duration health insurance by allowing consumers to buy plans providing coverage for any period of less than 12 months, rather than the current maximum period of less than three months."

These short-term plans are exempt from certain essential coverage standards—meaning they often don't cover healthcare related to pregnancy, substance abuse, or mental illness—and providers can deny coverage for pre-existing conditions as well as set limits on maximum annual and lifetime benefits for patients. Critics warn the expansion will only benefit healthy people at the expense of the most vulnerable Americans.

Acknowledging a series of actions by the Trump administration that were designed to attack the national healthcare system, Eagan Kemp, a policy advocate for Public Citizen, said the proposal "further sabotages healthcare in America by damaging insurance markets and allowing unethical insurers to offer false promises that place consumers at risk."

"This rule further destabilizes the Affordable Care Act (ACA) marketplaces by allowing insurers to offer junk plans targeting the young and healthy without essential health benefits. As a result, only the sick will be covered under plans with full ACA protections, driving up the costs of those plans and potentially making them unaffordable," he explained.

"By allowing the sale of plans that offer only the illusion of coverage," Kemp added, "more Americans will face unmet healthcare needs and many will face medical bankruptcy when they get sick and their plan does not cover the care they need."

Calling the move Trump's "biggest assault to the ACA, American families, and the law" yet, Andy Slavitt, who oversaw the Centers for Medicare and Medicaid Services during the Obama administration, noted that while "2017 Trump aimed for a vote to repeal the ACA," which failed multiple times, "2018 Trump is just skipping the voting part and ignoring the law."

Slavitt also outlined some of the likely consequences should the rule take effect, emphasizing that "all of this is by design."

Others pointed out that the Trump administration's ability to continuously undermine the ACA partly demonstrates why there is growing support for overhauling the nation's healthcare system and implementing a "Medicare for All" single-payer system that would make medical care a guaranteed right for all Americans.

1. Why are organizations opposed to repealing the ACA?

2. What solutions do they offer for the problems outlined in this piece?

"WASTED MEDICINE: A PRESCRIPTION FOR REDUCING WASTED HEALTH CARE SPENDING," BY MARSHALL ALLEN, FROM *PROPUBLICA*, DECEMBER 21, 2017

"A PROPUBLICA SERIES HAS ILLUSTRATED THE MANY WAYS THE U. S. HEALTH CARE SYSTEM LEAKS MONEY. HEALTH CARE LAEDERS AND POLICYMAKERS SUGGEST WAYS TO PLUG THE HOLES."

This story was co-published with NPR's Shots blog.
[Editor's note: Links can be found with the original article.]

Earlier this year, the Gallup organization set out to identify the top concerns everyday Americans have about money. Researchers asked more than a thousand people across the country, "What is the most important financial problem facing your family today?" Their top answer: the cost of health care.

Increases in medical costs have substantially outpaced economic growth for decades. In recent months, ProPublica has shown that it doesn't have to be this way. It's been estimated that the U.S. health care system wastes about $765 billion a year — about a quarter of what's spent. We've identified ways that tens of billions of dollars are being wasted, some of them overlooked even by many experts and academics studying this problem.

It's possible to reduce or eliminate some of the waste, but there are also formidable forces that benefit from it. Excess spending generates revenue and profit for what some have called the "medical industrial complex," said Dr. H. Gilbert Welch, professor of medicine at the Dartmouth Institute for Health Policy & Clinical Practice. "There are a number of people who can imagine ways to solve things," Welch said of the wasted spending. "But the political will and the forces at work can stop them pretty easily."

Still, wasting fewer health care dollars could drive down insurance premiums and out-of-pocket costs and maybe even free up resources for education, retirement and wage increases, among other things.

Here are the ways ProPublica found the medical industry is needlessly gobbling up money, along with steps health care leaders or policymakers say we could take right now to reduce the waste.

WHAT HOSPITALS WASTE

The nation's health care tab is sky-high. We're tracking down the reasons. First stop: a look at all the perfectly good stuff hospitals throw away.

What ProPublica found: Hospitals routinely toss out brand-new supplies and gently used equipment. Most of it goes to the dump, but some gets picked up by nonprofit organizations that ship the goods to the developing world.

How much money is wasted: No one tracks the total, but one charity in Maine had about $20 million worth of discarded goods filling its warehouses. Similar non-profits operate around the country. The University of California, San Francisco Medical Center studied how much it wasted during neurosurgery operations in one year. The discarded supplies were worth $2.9 million.

How to stop the squandering: UCSF reduced waste by reviewing the lists of supplies each surgeon wanted prepped for an operation. Many items could be taken off the lists. That reduced the number of supplies opened to set up each procedure, said Dr. R. Adams Dudley, director of the UCSF Center for Healthcare Value.

Hospitals could reduce wasted supplies by tracking everything thrown away, said Dr. Robert Pearl, former CEO of The Permanente Medical Group, the country's largest medical group and author of the book "Mistreated." The amount of waste could be reported when each patient is discharged, he said. Seeing the waste quantified would motivate people to prevent it, he said.

Several experts said paying hospitals a lump sum for everything involved in a particular procedure, instead of a la carte for each item, would mean they make more profit by cutting the amount of wasted supplies and equipment.

Read the story.

AMERICA'S OTHER DRUG PROBLEM

Every year nursing homes nationwide flush, burn or throw out tons of valuable prescription drugs. Iowa collects them and gives them to needy patients for free. Most other states don't.

What ProPublica found: Nursing home patients typically have their drugs dispensed a month at a time. So whenever a drug gets discontinued— if a patient dies, or moves out, or has a reaction — there's excess. Most nursing homes throw away the leftover drugs. They flush them down the toilet, put them in the trash or pay to have them incinerated. Iowa started a nonprofit organization to recover the excess drugs, inspect them and dispense them for free to patients.

How much money is wasted: It's estimated that hundreds of millions of dollars a year are wasted by throwing out nursing home medications. The CEO of a long-term care pharmacy in Florida said his company incinerates about $2.5 million in valuable medication every year. He estimated the total is $50 million statewide. Colorado officials said the state's long-term care facilities toss out 17.5 tons of potentially reusable drugs each year, worth about $10 million. Iowa is on pace to recover $6 million in drugs from nursing homes this year.

Other harm to the public: Flushing drugs down the toilet contaminates the water supply. Trace levels of pharmaceuticals have been detected in water throughout the country.

How to stop the squandering: Many states have laws that allow drug donation, but they have not invested in a program to help the process. ProPublica's story prompted lawmakers in Florida and New Hampshire to introduce legislation to create a program like Iowa's. Leaders in the Vermont medical community have also shown interest in starting a drug donation program.

Read the story.

HOW TWO COMMON MEDICATIONS BECAME ONE $455 MILLION SPECIALTY PILL

After I was prescribed a brand-name drug I didn't need and given a coupon to cover the out-of-pocket costs, I discovered another reason Americans pay too much for health care.

What ProPublica found: A drug company combined two over-the-counter drugs, naproxen, which goes by the brand name Aleve, and esomeprazole magnesium, also known as Nexium, to create a new pill called Vimovo. My doctor prescribed it to me. The company that makes it, Horizon Pharma, marketed the single pill as an innovation because it was easier to take one pill than two. A month's supply of the two inexpensive drugs costs about $40. The company billed insurance $3,252 for the Vimovo.

How much money is wasted: My insurance company rejected the bill, but Vimovo has net sales of more than $455 million since 2014. Horizon brought in $465 million more in net sales from a similar drug, Duexis, which combines ibuprofen and famotidine, aka Advil and Pepcid.

How to stop the squandering: Spurred by ProPublica's story, Connecticut now requires doctors to get prior authorization to prescribe Horizon's drugs to the 200,000 public employees, retirees and their dependents covered by a state insurance plan. The Connecticut comptroller also urged the attorney general's office to investigate Horizon's relationship with pharmacies and physicians. Other insurers have removed the drugs from their formularies.

Welch, the Dartmouth doctor, suggested tongue-in-cheek "warning labels" on drugs that aren't actually big innovations. In the case of Vimovo, the warning could say that the "specialty" pill is actually just a combination of two cheaper ingredients. "There may need to be public service advertisements that counter the advertising that says everything is the best thing since sliced bread," he said.

In cases where there are dramatic price increases, state lawmakers could require pharmaceutical companies to justify the higher costs, said Dr. Steven Pearson, president of the Institute for Clinical and Economic Review.

Secret deals and rebates currently cloak the actual price of drugs. Drug companies should have to publish the real prices of their products, said Linda Cahn, an attorney who advises corporations, unions and other payers on how to reduce their costs. Cahn recently proposed in an op-ed in The Hill what she calls a "bid day," where any drug company that wants to sell its products to Medicare beneficiaries would be required to submit the net cost of each medication. All the companies would be required to submit their price at the same time, say twice a year, and then stick with the price, which Medicare would make public for all to see. The bidding would inform consumers and force competition, she said. The same process could be used for all insurance plans, she said.

Read the story.

THE MYTH OF DRUG EXPIRATION DATES

Hospitals and pharmacies are required to toss expired drugs, no matter how expensive or vital. Meanwhile the FDA has long known that many remain safe and potent for years longer.

What ProPublica found: The term "expiration date" is a misnomer. The dates on drug labels are the point up to which pharmaceutical companies guarantee their effectiveness. But that does not mean the drugs are ineffective or dangerous the moment after they "expire." The Food and Drug Administration and Defense Department created the Shelf Life Extension Program to test the stability of drugs in the federal government's stockpiles and then extend their expiration dates, when possible. A 2006 study of 122 drugs tested by the program showed that two-thirds of them were stable every time a lot was tested. Each of them had their expiration dates extended, on average, by more than four years. But the same type of drugs in hospitals or pharmacies get thrown away when they "expire."

How much money is wasted: The total is unknown, but one mid-size hospital in Boston had to destroy about $200,000 in expired drugs in 2016. If hospitals nationwide throw out similar amounts of drugs annually, the total would be about $800 million trashed each year by hospital pharmacies alone.

Other harm to the public: Some expired drugs are in short supply and difficult to replace. On occasion, a pharmaceutical company will extend the expiration date of drugs for which there are shortages, but they are not required to do so.

How to stop the squandering: Drug companies could be required to do studies to determine how long their products actually last, and report the information, said Lee Cantrell, a pharmacist who helps run the California Poison Control System. Also, the government could publish data from the Shelf Life Extension Program, which is funded by taxpayers. The information would help people see "many types of medications are safe and effective much longer than their original expiration dates," Cantrell said.

Read the story.

DRUG COMPANIES MAKE EYEDROPS TOO BIG — AND YOU PAY FOR THE WASTE

The makers of cancer drugs also make vials with too much medication for many patients. The excess drugs are tossed in the trash — another reason health care costs are so high.

What ProPublica found: Drug companies make eyedrops much larger than what the eye can hold. That means patients pay for the excess from each drop, which runs down their cheeks. Vials of cancer drugs are also larger than necessary. The leftover cancer medication is billed to the patient — and thrown in the trash can.

How much money is wasted: It's unknown how much it costs to waste a portion of each eyedrop, but the industry is huge. Last year, drug companies brought in about $3.4 billion in the U.S. alone for dry eyes and glaucoma drops, according to the research firm Market Scope. A 2016 study estimated that, of the top 20 cancer drugs packaged in single-use vials, 10 percent of the medication is wasted, at a cost of $1.8 billion a year.

How to stop the squandering: Citing ProPublica's story, two U.S. senators introduced legislation that would require federal agencies to stop the waste associated with eyedrops and single-use cancer drug vials. Drugmakers could reduce the waste of cancer medication by making vials in varying sizes, so that less would be left over from each patient, said Dr. Peter Bach, director of the Center for Health Policy and Outcomes at Memorial Sloan Kettering Cancer Center in New York. Bach led a team that estimated the waste associated with vials of cancer drugs.

Read the story.

A HOSPITAL CHARGED $1,877 TO PIERCE A 5-YEAR-OLD'S EARS. THIS IS WHY HEALTH CARE COSTS SO MUCH.

An epidemic of unnecessary treatment is wasting billions of health care dollars a year. Patients and taxpayers are paying for it.

What ProPublica found: It's common for medical providers to deliver care that's not needed, or that costs more than necessary, and patients get stuck with the bills. In one case, a Colorado mom said her surgeon offered to pierce her daughter's ears as an add-on to a different operation. The mom agreed, assuming it would be free. But the hospital stuck her with a bill for $1,877 for "operating room services." ProPublica also highlighted unnecessary imaging tests, like extra mammograms and ultrasounds, and found it's common for hospital intensive care to be delivered to patients who are too sick or too healthy to benefit.

How much money is wasted: Unnecessary or needlessly expensive care wastes about $210 billion a year, according to the National Academy of Medicine. The cost of false-positive tests and overdiagnosed breast cancer is $4 billion a year, according to a 2015 Health Affairs study. Unnecessary intensive care costs about $137 million a year for about 100 hospitals in two states, one study estimated. That would put the tab of non-beneficial intensive care in the billions nationwide.

How to stop the squandering: Medicare has a fee schedule that sets prices and makes them public, said Welch, the Dartmouth physician who advocates against overtreatment. States could pass laws that establish similar fee schedules, he said, or insurance companies could implement them. Establishing set prices would reduce administrative overhead, he said, and allow patients to shop for the best deals.

Several experts said policymakers need to move medical providers from payment based on volume of services to payment based on value. Right now "fee for service" payment is common, so providers get a fee for everything they do. This gives them the incentive to do more, sometimes more than is necessary, or to provide care that's more expensive than it has to be. If providers were paid a lump sum to care for individuals or a group of patients, and the outcomes of their performance were measured to ensure quality didn't suffer, they would cut the waste. "You want to empower organizations to be responsible for improving patient health and reducing costs," said Dr. Elliott Fisher, director of The Dartmouth Institute for Health Policy and Clinical Practice.

Read the story.

1. How do inflated costs impact access to health care?

2. How does this article suggest getting these costs under control?

"HEALTH CARE IS A MESS ... BUT WHY?," BY SEAMUS COUGHLIN AND SEAN MALONE, FROM THE FOUNDATION FOR ECONOMIC EDUCATION, JULY 20, 2017

... AND IT DOESN'T HAVE TO STAY THAT WAY

You probably know a couple who both work full time to support their children, but even with their dual incomes, they're finding it more and more difficult to afford health insurance.

Everyday incidents like sports injuries, asthma, and blood pressure, combined with their anxiety over rising premiums, are turning their American dream into sleepless nights.

Why can't people catch a break? It wasn't always this way!

According to the Consumer Price Index and Medical-care price index from 1935 to 2009, the health care spending crisis didn't start until the mid 1960s, around the same time when Medicare and Medicaid were signed into law, and at the same time that we began requiring doctors to go through all sorts of expensive licensing procedures beyond medical school.

Since then, health care spending has doubled, even adjusted for inflation. Why? Well, there are a few reasons.

Everyone wants health care, but there's only so much to go around. And short supply leads to high prices. Normally what happens in a marketplace is that when prices are high, entrepreneurs try to profit by finding more affordable ways to provide goods and services.

The more people become involved in providing these services, the less scarce they become and the lower the prices drop, so that over time, more and more people can afford them.

This is what happened to televisions, microwaves, computers, cell phones, internet service, delivery services, food, shipping, transportation/air-travel, entertainment, home security, fitness, yoga, massages, and even all the medical technology, like LASIK, that isn't as heavily regulated or controlled by government.

CAN'T GOVERNMENT DRIVE DOWN THE PRICE OF GOODS AND SERVICES LIKE THE FREE MARKET?

Let's look at what happened with Medicare and Medicaid as an example. In 1965, these two single payer health insurance programs were instituted in the US. These programs made the unfortunate less dependant on impartial private charities and more dependant on political institutions and pharmaceutical companies.

On top of that, these programs constantly require tax increases, and because they function more to satisfy the health care industry than the worker, they continually lead to more expensive and wasteful ways of treating patients.

As a result, prices shot up, making it even more difficult for people to afford health insurance. Not only that, but in 1965, government took over the training of new doctors, and in 1997 they limited the number of new doctors they would train at 110,000 per year – and the number hasn't changed since!

Even worse, our government won't let migrant doctors from developed western countries practice in the US without undergoing this training. So, not only do experienced doctors from other countries not want to practice medicine here, but the ones who do are taking up 15% of those few 110,000 slots, limiting the supply of doctors even more.

WON'T OBAMACARE SOLVE THESE PROBLEMS?

Unfortunately, Obamacare suffers from similar problems. It eliminated the pricing structure by seriously restricting competition because all providers have to offer the same kinds of plans at the same price. And because that price isn't really determined by the market, providers can charge the taxpayer way more than they could otherwise. It's basically just a handout to big insurance companies.

But it doesn't have to be this way! If we get the government out of health care, more people like those you know will be able to get the care they need.

1. According to this article, what is the central issue facing health care access?

2. What barriers stand in the way of doctors entering medicine, and how does this impact access to services?

"AFFORDABLE CARE ACT'S PUSH TO CONSOLIDATE HEALTH CARE TO CURB COSTS MAY BACKFIRE," BY ERIC SUN, FROM *THE CONVERSATION*, JANUARY 6, 2016

In the United States, physicians practice medicine in a variety of settings, ranging from small solo practices to large, multispecialty group practices consisting of hundreds or even thousands of practitioners.

The tradition of the solo practitioner is one that is immediately familiar to most people, in part because this is the typical depiction of physician practice in movies and television shows.

However, this model of practice is falling by the wayside, and physicians are increasingly more likely to practice in the setting of large group practices. In 2008, only 18% of family practice physicians were employed in a solo practice, compared with 44% in 1986. This trend is being further encouraged by the Affordable Care Act on the grounds that larger practices can help curb costs by leading to better outcomes.

But will this physician consolidation actually lead to lower health care costs? The answer to this question has important consequences. Consolidation among physician practices has typically occurred via mergers between large health care systems.

Proponents of these mergers typically argue that they benefit patients, in large part because of their ability to reduce costs.

Are these claims too good to be true?

BENEFITS OF A LARGER PRACTICE

Larger practices can often offer many benefits for the physician, such as administrative support, interaction with colleagues and increased resources for professional development.

In addition, these large practices may benefit patients as well. Sometimes, bigger is indeed better, and large practices may be able to improve patient care and reduce costs by leveraging their size to implement large-scale measures aimed at quality improvement. For example, these groups may be able to more easily employ electronic medical record systems aimed at improving coordination of care, monitoring physician performance and reducing physician errors.

Indeed, these potential benefits form the rationale for many policies aimed at encouraging further consolidation among physicians.

For example, the Affordable Care Act encourages physicians to form large, multispecialty groups known as Accountable Care Organizations, in large part because of the belief that these organizations will be able to reduce costs by improving coordination of care.

However, a key question is whether these potential benefits may be outweighed by the potential disadvantages associated with large practices. Of crucial concern to antitrust authorities is that large practices may leverage their size to negotiate higher payments from insurers (and indirectly, patients), which could actually increase costs.

Simply put, a large practice is on much better ground than a solo practitioner to negotiate higher payments from a health insurers.

In a recent paper, we examined whether larger practices were associated with higher payments from private insurers in the case of orthopedic surgery and total knee arthroplasty, also known as "knee replacement."

KNEE-JERK REACTION

As a first step, we characterized the degree to which the provision of total knee arthroplasties in a given area was dominated by a single orthopedic surgery group or a small number of groups. Total knee arthroplasty is a good surgery to study because it is a commonly performed procedure whose use nearly doubled from 1991 to 2010.

We then examined whether insurers paid higher prices for total knee arthroplasty in markets dominated by a single group or a small number of groups.

Of course, markets that are dominated by a small number of groups may be associated with many other factors that could drive higher insurer payments. To address this possibility, rather than comparing prices across markets, our approach examined how changes in market structure were associated with changes in total knee arthroplasty payments within a given market over time.

In other words, our approach followed individual markets and asked how the payments in those markets changed over time as the provision of total knee arthroplasty became more (or less) dominated by a small number of groups.

CONSOLIDATION LEADS TO HIGHER COSTS

Overall, our results showed that payments were higher in markets dominated by a small number of groups.

In particular, insurer payments for total knee arthroplasty were 7% higher in the markets where the provision of total knee arthroplasty were most dominated by small number of groups, compared with markets where the provision of total knee arthroplasty was more spread out across groups.

To put this in context, this 7% increase is almost as large as the overall long-term decline in total knee arthroplasty payments we observed during the time period we studied (2001-2010).

POLICY IMPLICATIONS

Our results have several important policy implications.

First, they argue for some skepticism in evaluating the potential benefits of mergers between physician groups, as well as hospitals and health care systems more broadly.

While proponents of these mergers typically cite many of the potential benefits −such as the benefits discussed above − our research also suggests that these potential benefits may be outweighed by the ability of large providers to leverage higher payments from health insurers.

Second, our results suggest that antitrust authorities should closely evaluate whether any potential mergers may result in insurers (and patients) paying higher prices for medical services. For example, antitrust authorities should carefully consider the economic impact of the recently announced merger between Fairview Health and the University of Minnesota's health system.

At the end of the day, we are witnessing a large change in the way medical practice is being delivered, as the traditional model of solo practice gives way to a model in which physicians tend to practice in the context of larger organizations.

While the model has the ability to benefit patients and physicians, our study suggests that more work is also needed to understand its potential pitfalls

1. What are the pros and cons of medical service consolidation?

2. What recommendations does this article make for policy makers? How might these suggestions better serve those in need of health care services?

CHAPTER 6

WHAT ORDINARY PEOPLE SAY

In a debate that has been on-going for so long and at such a high level of coverage, it is easy to lose touch with the people most deeply impacted: the average citizens who seek access to health care under legislation passed by Congress. Their voices are often represented by legislators or advocacy groups, but it can still be difficult to get a sense of how individuals feel about policy or the health care system. Looking to those who have made their voices heard is a crucial way for us to have a sense of how health care looks and is experienced by citizens struggling to gain access to services and can help us understand how legislation impacts communities.

"TRUMP ISN'T LETTING OBAMACARE DIE; HE'S TRYING TO KILL IT," BY SIMON F. HAEDER, FROM *THE CONVERSATION*, JULY 28, 2017

Early on the morning of July 28, Republicans were dealt a surprising blow when Sen. John McCain (R-AR), along with Sen. Susan Collins (R-ME) and Sen. Lisa Murkowski (R-AK), voted against the latest installment of GOP efforts to repeal the Affordable Care Act (ACA).

In light of Republicans' failure to undo the ACA, President Trump was quick to react on Twitter, stating that he would simply "let ObamaCare implode" and have Democrats own the consequences. With Republicans holding all positions of power in Washington, D.C., these statements are startling by themselves.

However, with Congressional efforts in limbo, the Trump Administration seems to be going a step further than "letting" Obamacare fail. Indeed, it has emphasized an alternative strategy: actively sabotaging the Affordable Care Act.

CUTTING OUTREACH … AND MISDIRECTING IT

From the get-go, the Trump Administration quickly sought to impair the success of the Affordable Care Act. In one of its first moves, the Department of Health and Human Services under the direction of Secretary Tom Price pulled advertising for the federal government's enrollment entity, healthcare.gov.

The advertising has proven important to reach 18 to 34-years-olds. Enrolling these "young invincibles" is crucial for stabilizing risk pools because they are generally healthier and seek less medical care. States running independent campaigns, like California and its insurance marketplace Covered California, have been very successful in recruiting young people.

In an ironic twist, the Trump Administration used advertising funding intended for the promotion of the Affordable Care Act for a series of social media promotions attacking the law.

Also, in mid-July, the Administration moved to end contracts for enrollment assistance in 18 major cities. Contractors helped individuals navigate the often challenging enrollment process in such places as libraries, businesses and urban neighborhoods in these cities which had been identified by the Obama Administration as high priority.

Finally, the window for the next open enrollment period has been cut in half compared to previous years, thus making it difficult for time-pressed people and those who need enrollment help to enroll.

Many of these actions have triggered calls for inquiries into potential malfeasance by Congress and the Government Accountability Office (GAO).

SPREADING MISINFORMATION

Trump Administration officials have been actively traveling the countryand pushing talking points that are often false, or, at the very least, highly misleading and incomplete. Prominently featured in these efforts has been Vice President Mike Pence, who blamed Medicaid expansion for the backlog of disability cases in Ohio.

A favorite focus has been on increasing insurance premiums. While it is true that premiums have risen in many places, well over 80 percent of individuals purchasing insurance in the ACA marketplaces are eligible to receive premium subsidies that shield them from these costs.

Moreover, 59 percent of enrollees are also eligible to receive cost-sharing subsidies that shield consumers from rising out-of-pocket costs, another favorite Republican talking point.

Efforts to spread misinformation about the ACA has been coupled with equally misleading information about Republican repeal-and-replace efforts. For example, Republicans consistently argue that draconian reductions to the Medicaid program are not actual cuts, a position that virtually all health experts disagree with.

Republicans have repeatedly and persistently argued that the ACA is facing imminent implosion. Again, this position is in direct opposition to that of most health policy experts.

Trump Administration officials' preferred vehicle for outreach has been social media. For example, there has been a nearly constant stream on Twitter by HHS Secretary Tom Price focusing on "collapsing exchanges", rising premiums, and how the ACA is "wreaking havoc" on America. These claims are in direct contradiction to expert analyses or at very least incomplete and highly selective.

SPREADING UNCERTAINTY

Far from providing a major overhaul of the American healthcare and insurance system, the ACA provided a mere extension of the existing system, a system that relies extensively on private businesses to implement government policy.

Arguably, one of the most crucial components of the ACA is the active cooperation of insurance companies. And unlike with previous health reform efforts, insurance companies have been on board with Obamacare from the beginning.

Yet, insurance companies, both for-profits and non-profits, are first and foremost businesses that need to generate profits to stay afloat. Crucial in this endeavor is legal and regulatory certainty, which allows for long-term planning and helps guide investment decisions.

The constant undermining talk by the Trump Administration has done much to shake the confidence of insurance companies in the ACA. Entering a new market and spending resources to seek new enrollees require significant investments. Insurers do not want to see these potential investments wasted.

One of the most prominent issues in this regard has been the Administration's lack of commitment to paying the ACA's cost sharing subsidies. These subsidies help low-income consumers in the insurance marketplaces to shoulder out-of-pocket costs like co-payments for prescription drugs and doctor visits. Most importantly, the ACA requires insurers to cover these costs for their low-income enrollees. Insurers are then reimbursed by the federal government. Last year, reimbursements amounted to $7 billion.

Failure to pay these subsidies would be damaging to insurance markets. Insurers would still be required to make the payments for qualified individuals. However, they would not receive federal reimbursements. This would likely lead to massive premium increases as insurers are seeking to recover their payments. It could also potentially trigger an exodus by insurers.

Not surprisingly, given these uncertainties, insurance companies have left many markets and refused to enter new ones.

The situation is made worse by the Administration's announcement only days after taking office that it would not enforce the ACA's individual mandate and the associated tax penalty. While the Administration has reversed that decision for the 2016 tax year, it is unclear what will happen next tax season.

A FLAWED LAW DOESN'T MEAN IT'S HORRIBLE

As Minority Leader Chuck Schumer (D-NY) reightfully pointed out on the last day of the vote-arama on the Republican health care plan, Obamacare is not without its flaws. It does little to contain health care costs or improve the quality of health care provided in this country. Millions of Americans are left without insurance. Some parts of the country lack insurers.

Yet, undeniably, the ACA has done much good by providing coverage to more than 20 millions of Americans and added benefits to millions more.

Republican efforts in Congress to do away with the Obama Administration's signature accomplishment have been rather bumpy. While Republicans may still be successful, they have certainly taken much longer than President Trump's promise to repeal the ACA on Day One.

The verdict about the effectiveness of the Trump Administration's effort to actively undermine the ACA is still out. Yet the efforts appear deliberate and they have been ongoing since the Administration took over the White House and the Department of Health and Human Services.

Actively seeking to bring hardship to millions of Americans by sabotaging their health coverage is certainly highly questionable from a moral and ethical perspective. Future inquiries may also prove that they are illegal.

Perhaps most concerning, in my opinion, when the President of the United States and his closest advisers consistently spread false and misleading information, Americans are bound to lose. They may not only lose their health care coverage. They may also lose trust in their government and their elected leaders, and, eventually, in democratic government itself.

1. What evidence does the author of this article give for his claim that President Trump is fighting against the ACA?

2. What impact does this strategy have on our health care debate?

"IS HEALTH CARE A HUMAN RIGHT?," BY TREVOR BURRUS, FROM THE FOUNDATION FOR ECONOMIC EDUCATION, NOVEMBER 22, 2017

SAYING PEOPLE HAVE A RIGHT TO HEALTH CARE IS BASED ON A CONCEPTUAL CONFUSION.

Is there a right to health care? Most libertarians and classical liberals would say "no," and most progressives are shocked by that answer. For progressives, nothing could be more obvious than that everyone deserves access to health care regardless of their ability to pay. Distributing medical care based on wealth is for dystopian science fiction stories, where the underclass gets back-alley doctors and the ruling class gets sleek, modern hospitals. It doesn't belong in a civilized society.

Thus progressives ask, how can libertarians be so heartless as to not believe in a right to health care?

In this essay, I will try to answer that question. While I might not convince you that there isn't a right to health care, I hope to at least convey that, whatever a "right" to health care is, it is something fundamentally different from the sort of thing we usually call a "right"—so different, in fact, that we probably shouldn't be using the same word.

I'll be narrowly focused on that question. This essay is not about how the free market can solve health care, it's not arguing that health care isn't crucial to a flourishing life, and it doesn't claim that America's health care system is better than systems where people do have a "right" to health care. It's only about whether it makes sense to call health care a "right."

WHAT WE MEAN WHEN WE SAY, "RIGHTS"

In October 2017, the National Health Service, Great Britain's single-payer, socialized healthcare provider, announced that smokers and the obese would be banned from non-urgent surgery indefinitely. According to the *Telegraph*:

> [T]he new rules, drawn up by clinical commissioning groups (CCGs) in Hertfordshire, say that obese patients "will not get non-urgent surgery until they

reduce their weight"…unless the circumstances are exceptional.

The criteria also mean smokers will only be referred for operations if they have stopped smoking for at least eight weeks, with such patients breathalysed before referral.

The policy change understandably received significant criticism and brings to the fore the true meaning of "right" to health care.

What is a right? Even though "rights talk" permeates our political conversations, most people have never tried to define a right. Sometimes the term is used as a synonym for "important"—thus we hear about a right to clean water, shelter, education, and healthcare, all of which are undoubtedly important.

Yet having a "right" to something means more than that. Saying something is a "right" describes a relationship between individuals. It makes us think about our obligations to each other and the government's obligations to its citizens. Rather than focusing on *what* we have rights to, I'd like to focus on the *relationships* that a "right" creates and the distinction between positive and negative rights.

Rights describe a relationship between at least two people: a rightholder and a duty-holder. If someone has a right, others have a corollary duty. They're inextricably linked; two sides of the same coin.

Think of a desert island with only Robinson Crusoe, before Friday arrives. Crusoe could tell the trees and the animals that he has a "right" to life, but would it mean anything? A tiger chasing him through the grass is immune to Crusoe's right-claim. Tigers can't be duty-holders, so the term "right" does not describe a relationship between

Crusoe and the tiger. When Friday arrives, however, Crusoe's claim that he has a right to life implies something about the relationship between him and Friday. If Crusoe has a right to life, then Friday has a duty not to murder him, and vice versa.

The nature of the corollary duty is what distinguishes positive rights from negative ones. For negative rights, the corollary duty is an omission—that is, duty-holders are required to refrain from doing something, e.g. don't steal, don't punch people, don't kill. For a positive right, the corollary duty is a duty of action—that is, duty-holders are required to affirmatively act, e.g. provide food, provide health care, or provide resources for such things. Understanding this technical, but crucial, difference between positive and negative rights can help us identify four qualities that make them categorically different.

NEGATIVE RIGHTS ARE ABSOLUTE; POSITIVE RIGHTS ARE NOT

Negative rights can be enjoyed absolutely in a way positive rights cannot. Assuming no one is killing you (I hope), currently, you, the reader, are fully and absolutely enjoying your negative right to life. Similarly, if no one is stealing from you, assaulting you, or otherwise violating your body or your property then you are absolutely enjoying your negative rights to not be stolen from, assaulted, etc., and everyone else is absolutely fulfilling their negative duties.

Can positive rights can be enjoyed absolutely? It's difficult to imagine how. If there is a positive right to health care, how much health care does that entail?

When has the positive duty been fulfilled? If even one person enjoyed an absolute, positive right to health care, then, at least theoretically, every duty-holder would have to devote all of their time and resources to keep the right-holder alive for even one extra day. But that's ridiculous, and no one is claiming that. If not, however, then what are they claiming?

Most people would say that a "right" to health care guarantees some baseline care. They grant that because resources are limited, choices have to be made. Britain's NHS, for example, recently deemed six breast cancer drugs as "insufficient value for the money," even though some of the drugs had been shown to extend lives by months, if not years. And when the NHS decided to bar obese people and smokers from certain types of non-urgent surgery, those unfortunate cast-outs must have wondered, "I thought I had a right to health care." In fact, in a survey conducted in 2015, 75 percent of British doctors had seen care rationed, including the rationing of mental health care and knee and hip replacements. If you can get a knee or hip surgery in the U.K., the average waiting time is nearly a year compared to three to four weeks in the U.S.

Some argue that this question—how much health care do you have a right to?—can and should be answered by scientists, doctors, and policy experts, which is essentially how single-payer systems like the NHS deal with rationing. This raises a crucial and recurring point: *if "experts" are deciding how much health care someone receives, then the issue is being resolved by considerations other than the right-claim.* In other words, positive rights are inconclusive, in that they fail to answer our moral questions and, in fact, often just make them more difficult or insoluble.

The inconclusivity of positive rights makes them very different from negative rights. When someone claims a negative right to life, the corollary duties—who has them and what they have to do to fulfill them—are *fully answered by the right-claim*. While a claim to a negative right is sufficient to resolve an issue, a claim to a positive right merely inaugurates a conversation about other moral considerations. Should the young get more than the old? The skinny more than the obese? Is long-term pain amelioration, such as a back surgery, a better use of resources than giving a 95-year-old a few more weeks to live?

Obviously, because we don't have infinite resources, such decisions have to be made. But that very fact makes positive rights categorically different from negative rights. There's no plausible reason for politicians to consider taking away negative rights from entire classes of people—they couldn't, for example, proclaim that stealing from smokers or the obese is legal.

NEGATIVE RIGHTS ARE SCALABLE; POSITIVE RIGHTS ARE NOT

If you're fully enjoying your negative right to life, then every person on the planet is currently omitting killing you. If we doubled the population of the Earth tomorrow, it would be easy for every new person on the planet to omit killing you too. Someone can easily take on an infinite number of duties of omission and extend those duties to an infinite number of rightsholders. Doubling the population doesn't fundamentally change any question regarding who enjoys negative rights and who has a duty to respect them. The answer is simple: everyone and everyone, all the time.

The scalability of negative rights makes them truly universal rights. Negative rights make no distinctions based on citizenship, country of residence, or other forms of legal status. In fact, enjoying a negative right, properly conceived, requires no citizenship, legal status, or even government. True, it might be difficult to enforce your negative rights in the absence of a government, but that doesn't alter the moral status of your negative rights. Critics of the positive-negative distinction sometimes inappropriately conflate the cost of producing goods and services to satisfy positive-rights claims with the cost of police, courts, and prisons to punish infringements on negative rights, but that's a category error. "I'm entitled not to be stabbed," is a different matter than, "I'm entitled to have my attacker investigated and jailed."

Positive rights, in contrast, are not universal—they're conferred by virtue of one's legal status, such as citizenship. This means, as we've seen, they can be taken away or altered at the caprice of government officials, as was the case with Britain's obese and smokers. In 2009, under Massachusetts's "universal" health care system, 31,000 legal immigrants had their state-subsidized health insurance scaled back in order to counter budget shortfalls. While this might be required when resources are limited, it only underscores the fundamental difference between positive and negative rights.

NEGATIVE RIGHTS CAN EASILY EXIST TOGETHER; POSITIVE RIGHTS CANNOT

While people can take on an infinite number of duties to omission, they can only take on a finite number of duties to act. Positive rights, therefore, exist in an uneasy relationship with each other. If there is a "right" to healthcare, education, clean water, and even a vacation, then what happens when there is a conflict between two affirmative duties?

Recently, the European Union declared that traveling for vacation is a human right, and announced plans to subsidize travel for disadvantaged people. Yet there is also a right to health care in the European Union, so what happens when a doctor's right to go on vacation encounters a patient's right to health care? The conflict is never that direct, of course, but positive rights, by necessity, must conflict all the time.

Like the question of how much health care someone will receive, these conflicts are "solved" by policy experts and politicians. Once again, we see the invocation of a positive right failing to solve the moral question, ultimately just kicking it upstairs instead. Whereas negative rights can exist together simultaneously, positive rights form an uneasy and inconsistent tableau of mutually unsatisfiable claims. Philosophers, such as Hillel Steiner, have called this trait *compossibility*, or the ability to exist together. Whereas all negative rights are compossible, positive rights are incompossible.

NEGATIVE DUTIES ARE UNIVERSALLY SHARED; POSITIVE DUTIES ARE NOT

With negative rights, the corollary duties are equally shared by all duty-holders. No one is exempt from the obligation not to kill, steal, or assault. With positive rights, however, the corollary duties are not equally shared. As with the questions of who has a right to health care and how much do they get, we encounter further questions of who has to provide health care (or contribute to the provision) and how much they have to provide.

Again, whereas as negative right-claims require no additional moral considerations in order to determine who has a right, who has a duty, and what the nature and extent of that right/duty relationship, positive rights require secondary considerations in order to resolve the inevitable questions. Practically speaking, those questions are resolved by politics, and thus are subject to political winds.

POSITIVE "RIGHTS" ARE JUST POLITICALLY CONTINGENT CLAIMS TO SOMETHING

Negative rights are absolute, scalable, compossible, conclusive, and universal. Positive rights are not absolute, unscalable, incompossible, inconclusive, and restricted. Positive rights are something else entirely. It's difficult to come up with a precise term, but a positive right to health care is little more than a politically contingent claim to some health care, revocable and modifiable by morally irrelevant factors.

There's something deeply problematic about denying people health care based on extrinsic, contingent, morally irrelevant factors. When smokers made up a larger percentage of the British electorate, the NHS wouldn't have dreamed of denying them surgeries due to the political backlash they would have faced. Now, because smoking is becoming increasingly unpopular and morally charged among the ruling classes, smokers can be denied access to health care.

Some may say it is perfectly sensible that smokers are denied access due to their unwise decision to harm themselves while expecting others to pay for it. There is a right to health care, the argument goes, but no one has a right to make poor decisions and expect others to bear the costs.

This is a perfect example of the inconclusivity of positive rights. The initial claim to a right to health care only begins the inquiry into who, when, and how that right will be enjoyed. Smokers and the obese are being excluded based on a secondary moral limitation that exempts some people based on a political calculation, demonstrating that a positive right is less a *human* right and more a *political* one.

Moreover, in health-care systems like Britain's, all people are forced to pay for the NHS to some degree, and private medicine is a small, niche market because the NHS crowds out the alternatives. Smokers and the obese are largely unable to pay for their decisions themselves, even if they would prefer to. Perhaps some would like to exit the NHS so their health care options weren't determined by a political board, but there are few exit options available, especially at lower incomes.

Most important, however, is whether it is morally proper to deny people health care based on their membership in politically unpopular groups. Furthermore, even if it is proper, is it correct to call that a "right?" Such a question may seem easy when talking about those who are widely scorned, such as smokers and the obese, but what about homosexuals? During the 1980s, when AIDS swept through the homosexual community, some argued that they deserved their fate because they committed self-harm while expecting others to pay for it. During that time, and especially a decade before, it would have been very difficult for the gay community to muster up enough political support to protect their "right" to health care. Relying on politics seems fine until you're on the other side of it.

CONCLUSION

Astute readers might argue that allowing the market to "distribute" health care rests on equally morally irrelevant factors, primarily the ability to pay. I concede that point to a degree. This essay, however, is not about whether the market distributes health care in a morally justifiable way, but whether there is a positive right to health care.

If we can find no such right, it doesn't mean that healthcare is unimportant or that we don't have other moral obligations related to the health and well-being of our fellow citizens. I believe we have contingent moral obligations to help out those in need—contingent upon first being able to satisfy our other obligations. After you've put a roof over your head, provided for the care and well-being of your children and loved ones, and established some amount of security in your life, you have a moral obligation to help out those in need. That, however, is not a "right" to health care.

If health care is not a right, that's okay, because it's not the same as saying health care is unimportant. Rights, properly understood, explain the minimal normative obligations required for human beings to live together cooperatively rather than combatively. If you don't hit me, kill me, or steal from me, then I'll behave the same toward you, and we can thus be members of the same community based on a system of trust and mutual respect. Rights do not exhaust, however, the maximal normative obligations that may be required of us. That shouldn't bother us because rights can't do more than negatively prescribe our basic boundaries. By focusing on "rights to important things"—e.g. water, health care, education, shelter—the term is perverted and used to claim more than can be justified.

1. Why does the author argue that health care is not a right?

2. How does the author suggest we think about health care and how we ensure access to it?

"PROBLEMS OF U.S. HEALTH CARE ARE ROOTED IN THE PRIVATE SECTOR, DESPITE RIGHT-WING CLAIMS," BY MARK WEISBROT, FROM THE CENTER FOR ECONOMIC AND POLICY RESEARCH, JULY 20, 2011

A recent report by McKinsey and Company was seized upon by opponents of health care reform to create a new myth: that President Obama's health insurance reform (the 2010 Patient Protection and Affordable Care Act -- PPACA) will cause huge numbers of employers to drop health insurance coverage that they currently provide for employees.

The McKinsey study was soon shown to be worthless, and McKinsey itself acknowledged that it "was not intended as predictive economic analysis." But the myth seems to not be completely dead yet. For a more reasonable estimate of the impact of the health insurance reform, we can look to the non-partisan Congressional Budget Office. They estimated that the number of people (including family members) covered by employment-based insurance would be about 1.8 percent fewer in 2019, as a result of the PPACA legislation. Of course, this is more than counter-balanced by the fact that the percentage of the (non-elderly) population with insurance would increase from 82 to 92 percent – the main purpose of the reform.

Right-wingers, insurance companies, and other opponents of health care reform in the United States are always looking for ways to blame the government for the failures of our health care system. But the simple truth is that they have it backwards: our problems with health care are firmly rooted in the private sector. That is why the average high-income country – where government is vastly more involved in health care – spends half as much per person on health care as we do, and has better health outcomes.

That is why even Medicare – which has to pay for health care services and drugs at costs inflated by our dysfunctional private health care sector – has still proven to be much more efficient than private insurance. As Nobel Laureate economist Paul Krugman recently pointed out, from 1969 -2009, Medicare spending per person rose 400 percent, adjusted for inflation; private insurance premiums, also adjusted for inflation, rose 700 percent.

The most effective way to insure everyone and make our health care system affordable would have been to expand Medicare to everyone, while beginning the process of reducing costs through negotiation with, and restructuring incentives for, the private sector. The private insurance companies use up hundreds of billions annually on administrative costs, marketing, and other waste – which is what you would expect from companies who maximize profit by insuring the healthy and trying to avoid paying for the sick.

We also spend nearly $300 billion on pharmaceuticals each year, most of which is waste due to the patent monopolies of pharmaceutical companies. We could eliminate most of this waste through further public financing of pharmaceutical research, with new drugs sold as low-cost generics. Vermont Senator Bernie Sanders has introduced legislation in the Senate to realize these savings.

A distant second best reform, as compared with Medicare for all, would have been to include in Obama's health care reform a public option for employers and individuals to buy into. This would at least have provided some competition from a more efficient public sector to help control costs. But unfortunately, the insurance and pharmaceutical companies' lobbies proved to have a more powerful influence on our government than the voice of the people. This is another sad result of our dysfunctional health care system: The winners – waste for us is income for them – have a veto over health care reform.

It remains to be seen whether the PPACA will be a step toward more comprehensive, effective reform that gives us Medicare for all. In the meantime, the right will try to blame the government and the legislation itself for rising health care costs and other failures of our health care system. But in fact these result from the legislation not having gone far enough to rein in the private sector.

1. What impact does the author argue the private sector has on health care access?

2. What does the author argue about the role of politics and legislation in the relationship between health care and the private sector?

"THIS IS HOW YOU MAKE HEALTH CARE AFFORDABLE," BY JAY BOWEN, FROM THE FOUNDATION FOR ECONOMIC EDUCATION, AUGUST 4, 2017

THE CURRENT MODEL FOR DELIVERING HEALTHCARE IS UNSUSTAINABLE AND RAPIDLY HEADED FOR THE DREADED "DEATH SPIRAL."

Is the debate continues to rage in Washington, D. C., and around the country regarding the fate of Obamacare, one elegantly simple concept that would have a dramatic impact on healthcare costs is being drowned out by inflammatory rhetoric.

THE ONE AREA OF HEALTH CARE THAT'S DEFYING MASSIVE INFLATION

Out-of-pocket payment (OPP) by consumers for routine medical care would transform the system from one dominated by third party payers toward a model that would put consumers in charge of their healthcare dollars, and for the first time unleash market disciplines into the equation.

After all, we can all only imagine what our grocery carts would look like, not to mention our restaurant tabs, if a third party was paying for our food. Unfortunately, out-of-pocket payments have steadily trended down over the last 60 years and now account for only 10.5% of healthcare expenditures.

It is both stunning and disconcerting that the myriad of benefits that flow from a competitive, market driven system have never, in any substantial way, penetrated the healthcare and medical services arena. However, one striking exception to this competitive wet blanket is the $15 billion cosmetic surgery industry, the poster child for out of pocket payments, where innovation and price disinflation have been hallmarks for decades. Examples abound.

As Mark Perry has pointed out on his brilliant economic blog, Carpe Diem, over the past 19 years, the 20 most popular cosmetic procedures have increased at a rate 32% below the consumer price index (CPI) and 68% below the rate of medical services inflation.

Thus, the backbone of a productive reform plan must include a move away from third parties and employers controlling health care dollars toward individuals holding sway over their medical purse strings.

REMOVING CONSTRAINTS

This would mean that the "employer contribution" that currently is used to fund corporate group policies would transition to an increase in an employee's compensation, which would be funneled tax-free into a robust health savings account (HSA) that the employee would control for routine medical expenses.

As Michael Cannon of the Cato Institute has pointed out, "The employer contribution for health care is part of a worker's earnings and averages $13,000 per family. Yet the tax code gives control over that money to employers rather than the workers who earned it."

Importantly, this HSA would be paired with a high-deductible catastrophic policy and also be valid in the individual marketplace. Additionally, this would go a long way in helping to solve the portability issue that some employees face when changing jobs or careers.

Essential to making these individual plans more attractive and affordable would be the abolition of both the "community rating" and "essential health benefits" mandates currently embedded in Obamacare policies. These concepts make a mockery of a legitimate, actuarially sound insurance market by shifting costs from older and sicker people to younger and healthier people, thus promoting adverse selection.

Without these constraints, families could focus on basic and affordable policies that would better match their needs and also begin building a "rainy day health fund" via their HSA accounts.

Regarding both Medicaid and pre-existing conditions, a strong dose of old fashioned, Tenth

Amendment-oriented federalism is long overdue in dealing with these issues.

In fact, both from a philosophical and practical standpoint, they should never have come under the purview of the federal government and are best left to the individual states where diverse, vibrant, and innovative solutions could be implemented. This could include the establishment of reinsurance programs and high-risk pools for those with pre-existing conditions, and the phasing out of the open-ended federal entitlement status of Medicaid through a multi-year block grant program.

A PATIENT-CENTERED SYSTEM

The current third party payment/community rating model for delivering healthcare is unsustainable and rapidly headed for the dreaded "death spiral," which occurs when an escalation of sick people flock to the exchanges for insurance, while an increasing number of healthy people choose to leave the market. In fact, Aetna CEO Mark Bertolini has recently acknowledged as much.

Make no mistake, Obamacare was designed to invariably lead to a government-run, single-payer model, with its global budgeting, rationing of care, and long wait times for vital procedures in tow.

Without swift and decisive intervention with a system based on patient-centered choice and market mechanisms, the end result will be a Veterans Affairs (VA)-like model that would combine the worst aspects of government inefficiencies and substandard care.

A quick glance at the dismal state of Great Britain's National Health Service (NHS), Canada's single payer scheme, or our own insolvent Medicare and Medicaid plans provides Americans with an acutely unpleasant hint of what is in store if a single-payer model does indeed transpire.

1. What solutions does this author suggest for the high cost of health care?

2. What issues does this author see with single-payer health systems?

CONCLUSION

For decades, the question of how best to provide for the welfare of the American people has been a central debate in public and political spheres. Leaders, experts, advocates, and citizens have weighed in with statistics, policy initiatives, and personal experiences navigating the current healthcare market, giving us all a full sense of the scale and importance of health care in the United States. But as this collection has shown, there are no easy answers when discussing a system as complex and crucial as health care.

Our health care system has not been set in stone. It has evolved gradually over the past century, and continues to change today. From the introduction of programs like Medicaid and CHIP to the Affordable Care Act, the government has often been at the forefront of introducing new ways to provide for the most vulnerable in society. But the private sector—like insurance companies—also have a role in to play in shaping, designing, and testing new approaches to giving people the care they need. At the same time, it is important that we ensure that care is affordable, accessible, and not prohibited by things people can't help, such as their health history. All of these concerns come together to create a vibrant, sometimes heated debate in which we are all invested.

Health care is a need that all people share—like food and shelter, access to medicine and treatment are necessary for survival. This is part of why it is so hotly debated; we all want our loved ones to receive the care they need, and we will eventually need to go to a doctor. But while some feel it is best that the free market regulates health care, others feel the government has a duty to provide care through a single-payer program, with many wanting a system that bridges these two extremes. No matter our differences, we all want to make sure people in need of care receive it with little to no fear.

The United States health care system is unique in the world and is constantly changing. This makes it difficult to determine what the system might look like in ten or even twenty years. But any topic with such gravity is certain to continue being talked about, debated, and changed as we seek a better, more equal way to ensure our health care system is the best it can be.

BIBLIOGRAPHY

Allen, Marshall. "A Prescription for Reducing Wasted Health Care Spending." *ProPublica*, December 21, 2017. https://www.pro-publica.org/article/a-prescription-for-reducing-wasted-health-care-spending.

Bowen, Jay. "This is How You Make Health Care Affordable." Foundation for Economic Education, August 4, 2017. https://fee.org/articles/this-is-how-you-make-health-care-affordable.

Burrus, Trevor. "Is Health Care a Human Right?" Foundation for Economic Education, November 22, 2017. https://fee.org/articles/is-health-care-a-human-right/

Callaghan, Timothy. "Why the US Does Not Have Universal Health Care, While Many Other Countries Do." *The Conversation*, May 14, 2017. https://theconversation.com/why-the-us-does-not-have-universal-health-care-while-many-other-countries-do-77591.

Cliff, Betsy Q. "Explainer: Why Can't Anyone Tell Me How Much This Surgery Will Cost?" *The Conversation*, January 12, 2016. https://theconversation.com/explainer-why-cant-anyone-tell-me-how-much-this-surgery-will-cost-51013.

Conley, Julia. "Medicare for All Advocates Rip 'Cynical and Dishonest' Healthcare Initiative as Ploy at Undermine Single Payer." *Common Dreams*, February 7, 2018. https://www.commondreams.org/news/2018/02/07/medicare-all-advocates-rip-cynical-and-dishonest-healthcare-initiative-ploy.

Corbett, Jessica. "Continuing Sabotage of Americans' Healthcare, Trump Proposes Allowing Insurers to Offer 'Junk Plans'." *Common Dreams*, February 20, 2018. https://www.commondreams.org/news/2018/02/20/continuing-sabotage-americans-healthcare-trump-proposes-allowing-insurers-offer-junk.

Coughlin, Seamus and Sean Malone. "Health Care is a Mess … But Why?" Foundation for Economic Education, July 20, 2017. https://fee.org/resources/health-care-is-a-mess-but-why.

Dawson, Adrienne. "Reimagining the Future of America's Health Care System." Texas Enterprise at the University of Texas, May 3, 2017. http://www.texasenterprise.utexas.edu/2017/05/02/health-care/future-health-care-McClellan.

Haeder, Simon F. "Trump isn't Letting Obamacare Die; He's Trying to Kill It." *The Conversation*, July 28, 2017. https://theconversation.com/trump-isnt-letting-obamacare-die-hes-trying-to-kill-it-81373.

Kuhbander, Alexis and Kevin Cusack. "Arizona Organizations Urge Senate to Say No to New Healthcare Bill." *Cronkite News*, June 27, 2017. https://cronkitenews.azpbs.org/2017/06/27/arizona-organizations-urge-senate-to-say-no-to-new-healthcare-bill.

Ornstein, Charles. "We Fact-Checked Lawmakers' Letters to Constituents on Health Care." *ProPublica*, March 22, 2017 https://www.propublica.org/article/we-fact-checked-lawmakers-letters-to-constituents-on-health-care.

Shi, Leiyu. "The Impact of Primary Care: A Focused Review." Johns Hopkins Bloomberg School of Public Health, November 8, 2012. https://www.hindawi.com/journals/scientifica/2012/432892.

Staff. "Key Facts on the 'Repeal and Replace' Health Care Bill." *GovTrack*, March 9, 2017. https://govtrackinsider.com/key-facts-on-the-repeal-and-replace-bill-7f9ca20ce578.

Staff. "Remarks by the President on the Affordable Care Act." *Obama White House Archives*, October 20, 2016. https://obamawhitehouse.archives.gov/the-press-office/2016/10/20/remarks-president-affordable-care-act.

Staff. "Remarks by President Trump on Healthcare." *White House Press Office*, June 13, 2017. https://www.whitehouse.gov/briefings-statements/remarks-president-trump-healthcare.

Staff. "Remarks by the Vice President and Secretary Price at a Roundtable Discussion on Healthcare." *White House Press Office*, July 21, 2017. https://www.whitehouse.gov/briefings-statements/remarks-vice-president-secretary-price-roundtable-discussion-healthcare.

Trilling, David. "Survey Dissects U.S. Healthcare Spending Over the Decades." *Journalist's Resource*, January 12, 2017. https://journalistsresource.org/studies/government/health-care/health-care-spending-diabetes-heart-disease-back.

US Supreme Court. *National Federation of Independent Business v. Sebelius*, 567 U.S. 519 (2012). Cornell Law School: Legal nformation Institute, 2012. https://www.law.cornell.edu/supremecourt/text/11-393.

US Supreme Court. "Petition for a Writ of Certiorari to the United States Court of Appeals for the Eleventh Circuit: *United States Department of Health and Human Services, et al., Petitioners v State of Florida, et al.*" *Justice.gov*, September 15, 2014. https://www.justice.gov/sites/default/files/doj/legacy/2014/09/15/hhs-v-florida-petition-certiorari.pdf.

Weisbrot, Mark. "Problems of U.S. Health Care Are Rooted in the Private Sector, Despite Right-Wing Claims." Center for Economic and Policy Research, July 20, 2011. http://cepr.net/publications/op-eds-columns/problems-of-us-health-care-are-rooted-in-the-private-sector-despite-right-wing-claims.

CHAPTER NOTES

"THE IMPACT OF PRIMARY CARE: A FOCUSED REVIEW" BY LEIYU SHI

Due to the number of endnotes, they have not been included here. Please find them with the original article.

EXCERPT FROM "PETITION FOR A WRIT OF CERTIORARI TO THE UNITED STATES COURT OF APPEALS FOR THE ELEVENTH CIRCUIT: *UNITED STATES DEPARTMENT OF HEALTH AND HUMAN SERVICES, ET AL., PETITIONERS V STATE OF FLORIDA, ET AL.*" BY THE US SUPREME COURT

1. Amended by Health Care and Education Reconciliation Act of 2010, Pub. L. No. 111-152, 124 Stat. 1029.

2. Because the Affordable Care Act has not yet been codified in the United States Code, this brief will cite to the United States Code Annotated (U.S.C.A.) for ease of reference. All such citations are either to the 2011 Edition or the 2011 Supplement of the U.S.C.A.

3. The majority also declared the minimum coverage provision overinclusive because it "regulates those who have not entered the health care market at all." App. 119a. Congress is permitted to regulate categorically, without making exceptions for atypical individuals. *Raich*, 545 U.S. at 23. Assuming *arguendo* that there are individuals who go "from cradle to grave" without consuming health care, the group is "surely minuscule." App. 216a, 218a (Marcus, J., dissenting) (quoting States C.A. Br. 29). The two individual plaintiffs in this case (Brown and Ahlburg) do not disavow participation in the health care market; they simply state that they have not had health insurance for several years. Resp.'s Mot. for Summ. J. Exh. 25, Paras. 1, 5; *id.* Exh. 26, Paras. 1, 4. The theoretical existence of individuals who never obtain health care would not in

any event furnish a basis for invalidating the minimum coverage provision on its face.

4. Unlike most other forms of employee compensation, employer payments of health insurance premiums are generally excluded from an employee's income for purposes of both federal income tax and payroll taxes. See 26 U.S.C. 106. In addition, employers can deduct such premium payments as business expenses. 26 U.S.C. 162 (2006 & Supp. III 2009).

5. The court of appeals' Commerce Clause holding also conflicts with the views expressed by two members of the Fourth Circuit panel in *Liberty University*. Although that court found a constitutional challenge to the minimum coverage provision barred by the Anti-Injunction Act, see 2011 WL 3962915, at *4-*16, two members of the panel addressed the merits as well. See *id*. at *35-*47 (Davis, J., dissenting) (finding minimum coverage within commerce authority); id. at *16 (Wynn, J., concurring) ("I think that [Judge Davis's] position on the Commerce Clause is persuasive.").

6. One other case pending in a court of appeals squarely presents a constitutional challenge to the minimum coverage provision. See *Mead v. Holder*, 766 F. Supp. 2d 16 (D.D.C. 2011), appeal pending sub nom. *Seven-Sky v. Holder*, No. 11-5047 (D.C. Cir. argued Sept. 23, 2011). In several other cases, courts of appeals have concluded that plaintiffs lacked standing to challenge the minimum coverage provision. See *Virginia ex rel. Cuccinelli v. Sebelius*, No. 11-1057, 2011 WL 3925617 (4th Cir. Sept. 8, 2011); *Baldwin v. Sebelius*, No. 10-56374, 2011 WL 3524287 (9th Cir. Aug. 12, 2011); *New Jersey Physicians, Inc. v. President of the United States*, No. 10-4600, 2011 WL 3366340 (3d Cir. Aug. 3, 2011); see also *Kinder v. Geithner*, No. 10-cv-00101, 2011 WL 1576721 (E.D. Mo. Apr. 26, 2011) (dismissing on standing grounds), appeal pending, No. 11-1973 (8th Cir. oral argument scheduled for Oct. 20, 2011).

7. If the Court grants a certiorari petition filed by the plaintiffs in *Liberty University* to challenge the Fourth Circuit's holding in that case, the Court could instead rely on briefing in that case to address the Anti-Injunction Act issue, perhaps appointing an amicus to defend the Fourth Circuit's judgment in that case. The respondents in this case could then file amicus briefs on the Anti-Injunction Act in *Liberty University*.

GLOSSARY

Affordable Care Act (ACA) — The 2010 legislation that introduced sweeping reforms to the health care system, including restrictions on insurance companies and an individual mandate.

American Health Care Act (AHCA) — A bill introduced to Congress in 2017 that partially repeals the ACA while maintaining some parts of the law.

Children's Health Insurance Program (CHIP) — An insurance program covering health care costs for young people and children with low-incomes.

deductible — The amount of money an individual or family is required to spend on health care costs in a given year before insurance coverage begins paying all or part of their incurred costs.

health care — Medical services, including preventative and emergency care, and the way in which we access those services.

health care system — An umbrella term for care providers, insurance companies, and other groups that are involved in administering health care and the laws under which they function.

health market exchanges — Systems introduced by the ACA and run by the states that allow individuals to shop for insurance coverage by comparing plans directly.

hyperbole — Overstating or misrepresenting the facts by inflating the sense of danger or impact.

individual mandate — The requirement under the ACA that all citizens have insurance coverage.

insurance companies — Privately held companies that provide plans that cover all or parts of healthcare costs, based on guidelines and restrictions.

Medicaid — A state-run, government-funded program that covers health care costs for low-income families and individuals.

Medicare—Insurance program for citizens aged sixty-five or older, and for some under that age with chronic illness or disabilities.

out-of-pocket—Costs that are not covered by insurance, and have to be paid by an individual directly.

partisan—Closely aligned with one political party, with strong opposition in the other.

preexisting conditions—Medical conditions or treatments that are taken into account during the insurance screening process, and for which people could be denied coverage before implementation of the ACA.

self-insure—Going without coverage through a company or program in favor of covering all health care costs out-of-pocket.

FURTHER READING

BOOKS

Brownlee, Shannon. *Overtreated: Why Too Much Medicine Is Making Us Sicker and Poorer.* New York, NY: Bloomsbury USA, 2010.

Buchbinder, Mara et al. *Understanding Health Inequalities and Justice.* Chapel Hill, NC: The University of North Carolina Press, 2016.

Cohn, Jonathan. *Sick: The True Story of How America's Health Care Crisis.* New York, NY: HarperCollins, 2009.

Gillick, Muriel R. *Old and Sick in America: The Journey Through the Health Care System.* Chapel Hill, NC: The University of North Carolina Press, 2017.

Goldhill, David. *Catastrophic Care: Why Everything We Think We Know about Health Care Is Wrong.* New York, NY: Vintage, 2013.

Rawal, Purva H. *The Affordable Care Act: Examining the Facts.* Santa Barbara, CA: ABC-CLIO, 2016.

Reid, T. R. *The Healing of America: A Global Quest for Better, Cheaper, and Fairer Health Care.* New York, NY: Penguin, 2010.

Richmond, Julius B. et al. *The Health Care Mess: How We Got Into It and What It Will Take To Get Out.* Cambridge, MA: Harvard University Press, 2007.

Shaw, Greg M. *The Healthcare Debate.* Santa Barbara, CA: Greenwood, 2010.

Smith, David Barton. *The Power to Heal: Civil Rights, Medicare, and the Struggle to Transform America's Health Care System.* Nashville, TN: Vanderbilt University Press, 2016.

WEBSITES

Brookings Institute Center for Health Policy
https://www.brookings.edu/center/center-for-health-policy
This think tank, based in Washington, DC, is focused on
American health care delivery. Its website includes research used
by the institute to advocate for innovative health care strategies.

US Department of Health and Human Services
https://www.hhs.gov
This federal agency is responsible for implementing health policy,
making recommendations to legislators, and carrying out research
related to health care services and issues.

INDEX

ABOUT THE EDITOR

Bridey Heing is a writer and book critic based in Washington, DC. She holds degrees in political science and international affairs from DePaul University and Washington University in Saint Louis. Her areas of focus are comparative politics and Iranian politics. Her master's thesis explores the evolution of populist politics and democracy in Iran since 1900. She has written about Iranian affairs, women's rights, and art and politics for publications like the *Economist*, *Hyperallergic*, and the *Establishment*. She also writes about literature and film. She enjoys traveling, reading, and exploring Washington, DC's many museums.